MATE

compiled by
LEXUS

RICHARD DREW PUBLISHING
Glasgow

RICHARD DREW PUBLISHING LTD
6 Clairmont Gardens
Glasgow G3 7LW
Scotland

First Published 1984
New Edition 1988

ISBN 0 86267 215 5

Typeset by Morton Word Processing Ltd.,
Scarborough, North Yorkshire
Printed in Great Britain by
Cox & Wyman Ltd.

CONTENTS

LA FRANCE

0   km   200

L'ECOSSE
Glasgow

L'ANGLETERRE

LE PAYS
DE GALLES

LA MER DU NORD

LA HOLLANDE
Amsterdam

Rhin

L'ALLEMAGNE

Londres
Douvres
Calais
Boulogne
Dieppe

Ostende
Bruxelles
Lille
LA BELGIQUE
Liège

Bonn

Luxembourg

LA MANCHE

Cherbourg
Le Havre
Caen
Rouen
Seine
Reims
Metz

Rhin

Brest

Rennes

Paris
Nancy
Strasbourg

Orléans

Tours

Loire

Dijon

Besançon

Bâle
Berne

Nantes

Poitiers

La
Rochelle
Limoges
Clermont-
Ferrand

Lyon
Lausanne
Genève
LA SUISSE
Les Alpes
L'ITALIE

LE GOLFE
DE
GASCOGNE

Bordeaux

Saint-
Etienne

Grenoble
Turin

Bayonne
Biarritz
Toulouse
Pau

Nîmes
Montpellier
Rhône
Avignon
Cannes
Nice
Marseille
Côte d'Azur

Pyrénées

L'ESPAGNE

Barcelone

LA MÉDITERRANÉE

LA
CORSE
Ajaccio

Madrid

FRENCH

Special sounds in the pronunciation guide:

j   is like the second sound in 'measure' or 'seizure'

o̅n̅, a̅n̅ are the typical French nasal sounds

uh   is pronounced as in 'a' or the u in 'butter'

Feminine forms, where noticeably different from masculine forms, are given in brackets.

bon voyage!

....

a, an un (une) [an, oon]
accident un accident [axee-don]
adaptor un adaptateur [ahdap-tah-tur]
address une adresse [ah-dress]
after après [ah-pray]
afternoon l'après-midi [ahpray-mee-dee]
   good afternoon bonjour [bon-joor]
again de nouveau [duh noo-voh]
airport l'aéroport [ah-ayroh-por]
all tout [too]
   it's all right, I'm all right ça va [sah vah]
   all day toute la journée [toot lah joor-nay]
almost presque [presk]
alone seul [surl]
always toujours [too-joor]
and et [ay]
another un/une autre [an/oon ohtr]
   another beer, please encore une bière, s'il
   vous plaît [on-kor oon bee-yair seel voo play]
arrive arriver [ahree-vay]
ashtray un cendrier [sondree-yay]
ask demander [duh-mon-day]
baby un bébé [bay-bay]
back: I'll be back je reviens [juh ruhv-yan]
bad mauvais [moh-vay]
bag un sac
bank une banque [bonk]
bar un bar
bath un bain [ban]
bathroom la salle de bain [sahl duh ban]
beach une plage [plahj]
beautiful beau (belle) [boh, bel]
because parce que [pahrsuh-kuh]
bed un lit [lee]
beer de la bière [bee-yair]
before avant [ah-von]
best: the best ... le meilleur ... [may-yur]
better meilleur [may-yur]
bicycle une bicyclette [bee-see-klet]
big grand [gron]

bill l'addition [ahdees-yon]
black noir [nwahr]
blanket une couverture [koovair-toor]
blue bleu [bluh]
boat un bateau [bah-toh]
book un livre [leevr]
boring ennuyeux [on-nwee-yuh]
both les deux [lay duh]
bottle une bouteille [boo-tay]
boy un garçon [gar-son]
brakes les freins [fran]
bread du pain [pan]
breakfast le petit déjeuner [puhtee dayjur-nay]
broken: it's broken c'est cassé [say kah-say]
brother: my brother mon frère [frair]
bus l'autobus [otoh-booss]
bus stop l'arrêt d'autobus [ahray ...]
butter du beurre [bur]
café un café [kah-fay]
camera un appareil-photo [appah-ray ...]
campsite un terrain de camping [tay-ran duh kon-peeng]
can: can I have ...? est-ce que je peux avoir ...? [eskuh juh puh ah-vwahr]
   can you ...? est-ce que vous pouvez ...? [eskuh voo poo-vay]
   I can't ... je ne peux pas ... [juh nuh puh pah]
cancel annuler [ahnoo-lay]
car une voiture [vwah-toor]
car park un parking
centre le centre [sontr]
change changer [shon-jay]
   could you change this into francs? est-ce que vous pouvez me changer ça en francs? [eskuh voo poo-vay muh shon-jay sah on fron]
cheap bon marché [bon mahr-shay]
cheers! santé! [son-tay]
cheese du fromage [froh-mahj]
chemist's une pharmacie [farmah-see]
cheque un chèque [shek]

....

children les enfants [on-fon]
chips des frites [freet]
chocolate du chocolat [shokoh-lah]
church une église [ay-gleez]
cigar un cigare [see-gar]
cigarette une cigarette [seegah-ret]
clean propre [prohpr]
clothes les vêtements [vet-mon]
coat un manteau [mon-toh]
coffee un café [kah-fay]
   a white coffee/a black coffee un café au
   lait/un café [... oh lay]
cold froid [frwah]
comb un peigne [pen]
come venir [vuh-neer]
   come in! entrez [on-tray]
constipation la constipation [konstee-pah-syon]
consul le consul [kon-sool]
cost: what does it cost? combien ça coûte?
   [konb-yan sah koot]
could: could you ...? est-ce que vous pouvez ...?
   [eskuh voo poo-vay]
   could I have ...? est-ce que je peux avoir ...?
   [eskuh juh puh ah-vwahr]
crazy fou (folle) [foo (fol)]
crisps des chips [chips]
Customs la douane [dwahn]
daughter: my daughter ma fille [fee]
delicious délicieux [daylees-yuh]
dentist un dentiste [don-teest]
develop: could you develop these? est-ce que
   vous pouvez me développer ces films? [eskuh
   voo poo-vay muh dayv-loh-pay say feelm]
different différent [deefay-ron]
difficult difficile [deefee-seel]
dinner le dîner [dee-nay]
do faire [fair]
   how do you do? enchanté [on-shon-tay]
doctor un docteur [dok-tur]
door la porte [pohrt]

dress une robe [rohb]
drink: something to drink quelque chose à
  boire [kelkuh shohz ah bwahr]
driving licence le permis de conduire [pair-mee
  duh kōn-dweer]
drunk ivre [eevr]
dry-clean nettoyer à sec [naytwah-yay ah sek]
early tôt [toh]
easy facile [fah-seel]
eat: something to eat quelque chose à manger
  [kelkuh shohz ah mōn-jay]
else: something else quelque chose d'autre
  [kelkuh-shobz dohtr]
England l'Angleterre [ōngluh-tair]
English anglais [ōn-glay]
enough assez [ah-say]
entertainment les attractions [ahtraks-yōn]
evening le soir [swahr]
  good evening bonsoir [bōn-swahr]
everyone tout le monde [too luh mōnd]
everything tout [too]
excellent excellent [ayksay-lōn]
excuse me pardon [pahr-dōn]
expensive cher [shair]
far: is it far? c'est loin? [say lwān]
fast rapide [rah-peed]
  don't speak so fast ne parlez pas si vite [nuh
  pahr-lay pah see veet]
father: my father mon père [pair]
few: a few days quelques jours [kel-kuh joor]
film un film [feelm]
first premier [prum-yay]
food la nourriture [nooree-toor]
for pour
fork une fourchette [foor-shet]
France la France [frōns]
free libre [leebr]; (*non-paying*) gratuit
  [grah-twee]
French français [frōn-say]
Friday vendredi [vōndruh-dee]

....

friend un ami [ah-mee]
from de [duh]
fun: it's fun c'est amusant [sayt ahmoo-zōn]
funny drôle [drohl]
garage un garage [gah-rahj]
girl une fille [fee]
give donner [doh-nay]
glasses: my glasses mes lunettes [loo-net]
go aller [ah-lay]
    I'm going there tomorrow j'y vais demain [jee vay duh-mān]
    he's gone il est parti [eelay pahr-tee]
good bon [bōn]
goodbye au revoir [oh ruh-vwahr]
guide un guide [gheed]
hairdresser's un coiffeur [kwah-fur]
handbag un sac à main [... ah mān]
happy heureux [ur-ruh]
harbour le port [pohr]
hard dur [door]
have avoir [ah-vwahr]
    do you have ...? avez-vous ...? [ah-vay voo]
    we have ... nous avons [nooz ah-vōn]
    I don't have ... je n'ai pas ... [juh nay pah]
he il [eel]
    is he ...? est-ce qu'il est ...? [eskeel ay ...]
headache un mal de tête [mal duh tet]
hello bonjour [bōn-joor]
help: can you help me? est-ce que vous pouvez m'aider? [eskuh voo poo-vay may-day]
her: with her avec elle [... el]
    her bag/car son sac/sa voiture [sōn ...]
here ici [ee-see]
him: with him avec lui [... lwee]
his son [sōn], sa [sah], (*plural*) ses [say]
holiday les vacances [vah-kōns]
home: at home chez moi [shay mwah]
hospital un hôpital [ohpee-tal]
hot chaud [shoh]; (*spiced*) fort [fohr]
hotel un hôtel [oh-tel]

....

hour une heure [ur]
house une maison [may-zōn]
how? comment? [koh-mōn]
   how are you? comment allez-vous? [kon-mōnt ah-lay voo]
   how many? how much? combien? [kōnb-yan]
hungry: I'm hungry/not hungry j'ai faim/je n'ai pas faim [jay fān, juh nay pah fān]
hurt: it hurts ça fait mal [sah fay mal]
husband: my husband mon mari [mōn mah-ree]
I: I am je suis [juh swee]; **I have** j'ai [jay]
ice de la glace [glahs]
ice cream une glace [glahs]
if si [see]
ill malade [mah-lad]
immediately tout de suite [toot sweet]
important important [ānpohr-tōn]
in dans [don]; **in France** en France [ōn ...]
Ireland l'Irlande [eer-lōnd]
it: it is ... c'est ... [say]
   is it ...? est-ce que c'est ...? [eskuh say]
jacket une veste [vest]
just: just a little juste un petit peu [joost ān puh-tee puh]
key la clé [klay]
kiss embrasser [ōnbrah-say]
knife un couteau [koo-toh]
know: I don't know je ne sais pas [juh nuh say pah]
last dernier [dairn-yay]
   last night hier soir [yair swahr]
late tard [tahr]; **later** plus tard [ploo tahr]
   see you later à tout à l'heure [ah toot ah lur]
leave: we're leaving tomorrow nous partons demain [noo pahr-tōn duh-mān]
   when does the bus leave? quand est-ce que le bus part? [kōnteskuh luh boos pahr]
   I left two shirts in my room j'ai laissé deux chemises dans ma chambre [jay lay-say ...]

....

can I leave this here? est-ce que je peux
laisser ça ici? [eskuh juh puh lay-say sah ee-see]
left: on the left à gauche [ah gohsh]
left luggage la consigne [kōn-seen]
letter une lettre [letr]
light la lumière [loom-yair]
  do you have a light? est-ce que vous avez du
feu? [eskuh vooz ah-vay doo fuh]
like: would you like ...? est-ce que vous
  voulez ...? [eskuh voo voo-lay]
  I'd like ... j'aimerais ... [jaym-ray]
  I like it ça me plaît [sah muh play]
  I don't like it ça ne me plaît pas
little petit [puh-tee]
  a little un peu [ān puh]
lorry un camion [kahm-yōn]
lose: I've lost ... j'ai perdu ... [jay pair-doo ...]
  I'm lost je me suis perdu [juh muh swee]
lot: a lot (of) beaucoup (de) [boh-koo duh]
  not a lot pas beaucoup [pah ...]
luggage les bagages [bah-gah]
lunch le déjeuner [day-jur-nay]
main road la route/rue principale [root, roo
  prānsee-pal]
man un homme [om]
  the man at the desk le monsieur au guichet
  [luh muhs-yuh oh ghee-shay]
manager le directeur [deerek-tur]
map une carte [kart]
  a map of Paris un plan de Paris [ān plōn duh
  pah-ree]
market un marché [mahr-shay]
match: a box of matches une boîte d'allumettes
  [bwaht dahloo-met]
matter: it doesn't matter ça ne fait rien [sah nuh
  fay ree-yah]
maybe peut-être [puht-aitr]
me: for me pour moi [poor mwah]
mean: what does that mean? qu'est-ce que ça
  veut dire? [keskuh sah vuh deer]

....

menu la carte [kart]
milk du lait [lay]
mineral water de l'eau minérale [oh
  meenay-rahl]
minute une minute [mee-noot]
Monday lundi [lan̄-dee]
money l'argent [ahr-jōn̄]
more plus [ploo(s)]
  more wine, please encore du vin, s'il vous
  plaît [ōn̄-kor doo van̄ seel voo play]
morning le matin [mah-tan̄]
  good morning bonjour [bōn̄-joor]
mother: my mother ma mère [mair]
motorbike une moto [moh-toh]
motorway l'autoroute [otoh-root]
mountain une montagne [mōn̄-tan]
much beaucoup [boh-koo]
  not much pas beaucoup [pah ...]
music la musique [moo-zeek]
must: I must go je dois partir [juh dwah
  pahr-teer]
  we must not ... nous ne devons pas ... [noo nuh
  duh-vōn̄ pah]
  you must ... vous devez ... [voo duh-vay]
my mon [mōn̄], ma [mah], (*plural*) mes [may]
name un nom [nōn̄]
  my name is ... je m'appelle ... [juh mah-pel]
  what's your name? quel est votre nom?
  [kel-ay vohtr nōn̄]
near près (de) [pray (duh)]
necessary nécessaire [naysay-sair]
needle une aiguille [ay-gwee]
never jamais [jah-may]
new nouveau (nouvelle) [noo-voh, noo-vel]
newspaper un journal [joor-nal]
next prochain [pro-shan̄]
nice (*nice-looking*) joli [joh-lee]
  (*pleasant, kind*) gentil [jōn̄-tee]
night la nuit [nwee]
  good night bonne nuit [bon nwee]

....

no (*reply*) non [nōn]
  no money pas d'argent [pah dahr-jōn]
nobody personne [pair-son]
noisy: our room is too noisy notre chambre est
  trop bruyante [... shōnbr ay troh brwee-yōnt]
not pas [pah]
  not me/that one pas moi/celui-là
  I don't smoke je ne fume pas [juh nuh ... pah]
nothing rien [ree-yān]
now maintenant [mānt-nōn]
nowhere nulle part [nool pahr]
number le numéro [noomay-roh]
of de [duh]
often souvent [soo-vōn]
oil de l'huile [weel]
OK d'accord [dah-kor]
  it's O.K. ça va [sah vah]
old vieux (vieille) [vee-yuh, vee-yay]
on sur [soor]
one un (une) [ān, oon]
only seulement [surl-mōn]
open ouvert [oo-vair]
or ou [oo]
orange juice un jus d'orange [jou doh-rōnj]
other autre [ohtr]
our notre [nohtr], (*plural*) nos [noh]
over: over here ici [ee-see]
  over there là-bas [lah-bah]
painkillers des calmants [kal-mōn]
paper du papier [pahp-yay]
pardon? pardon? [pahr-dōn]
passport le passeport [pass-pohr]
pen un stylo [stee-loh]
people les gens [jōn]
petrol de l'essence [ay-sōns]
photograph une photo
piece un morceau [mohr-soh]
plane un avion [ahv-yōn]
platform: which platform? quel quai? [kel kay]
please s'il vous plaît [seel voo play]

....

police la police [poh-lees]
pool (*swimming*) une piscine [pee-seen]
possible possible [poh-seebl]
postcard une carte postale [... pohs-tahl]
post office la poste [posst]
pretty joli [joh-lee]
problem un problème [proh-blem]
pronounce: how do you pronounce that?
  comment est-ce que ça se prononce? [koh-mōnt
  eskuh sah suh proh-nōns]
purse un porte-monnaie [port-moh-nay]
quiet tranquille [trōn-keel]
quite (*fairly*) assez [ah-say]
rain: it's raining il pleut [eel pluh]
ready: when will it be ready? ce sera prêt
  quand? [suh serah pray kōn]
receipt une quittance [kee-tōns]
red rouge [rooj]
rent: can I rent a car? est-ce que je peux louer
  une voiture? [eskuh juh puh loo-ay ...]
repair: can you repair it? est-ce que vous
  pouvez le réparer? [eskuh voo poo-vay luh
  raypah-ray]
reservation une réservation [rayzair-vahs-yōn]
restaurant un restaurant [restoh-rōn]
return: a return to ... un aller–retour pour ... [ān
  ahlay ruh-toor poor]
right: on the right à droite [ah drwaht]
  that's right c'est juste [say joost]
river une rivière [reev-yair]
road une route [root]; (*in town*) une rue [roo]
room une chambre [shōnbr]
  do you have a single/double room? est-ce
  que vous avez une chambre pour une
  personne/deux personnes? [eskuh vooz ah-vay
  oon shōnbr poor oon pair-son ...]
  for one night/two nights pour une nuit/deux
  nuits [poor oon nwee, duh nwee]
safe sans danger [sōn dōn-jay]
salt le sel

....

same le (la) même [mem]
  same again la même chose [lah mem shohz]
Saturday samedi [sam-dee]
say: how do you say in French ...? comment
  est-ce qu'on dit en français ...? [koh-mont eskon
  dee on fronn-say]
  what did he say? qu'est-ce qu'il a dit?
  [kes-keel ah dee]
scissors une paire de ciseaux [pair duh see-zoh]
Scotland l'Ecosse [ay-koss]
sea la mer [mair]
seat une place [plahs]
see: I see je vois [juh vwah]
  can I see the room? est-ce que je peux voir la
  chambre? [eskuh juh puh vwahr lah shonbr]
send envoyer [onvwah-yay]
shampoo un shampooing [shon-pwan]
she elle [el]
  is she ...? est-ce qu'elle est ...? [eskel ay]
shirt une chemise [shuh-meez]
shoes des chaussures [shoh-soor]
shop un magasin [mahgah-zan]
show: show me montrez-moi [mon-tray mwah]
shower une douche [doosh]
shut fermé [fair-may]
single: a single to ... un billet aller pour ... [an
  bee-yay ahlay poor]
sister: my sister ma soeur [sur]
sit: can I sit here? est-ce que je peux m'asseoir
  ici? [eskuh juh puh mah-swahr ee-see]
skirt une jupe [joop]
slow lent [lon]
small petit [puh-tee]
so si [see]
  not so much pas tant [pah ton]
soap un savon [sah-von]
somebody quelqu'un [kel-kan]
something quelque chose [kel-kuh shohz]
son: my son mon fils [fees]
soon bientôt [bee-yan-toh]

sorry: I'm sorry excusez-moi [exkoo-zay-mwah]

souvenir un souvenir [soov-neer]

speak: do you speak English? est-ce que vous parlez anglais? [eskuh voo par-lay ōn-glay]

I don't speak French je ne parle pas français [juh nuh parl pah frōn-say]

spoon une cuillère [kwee-yair]

stairs les escaliers [eskahl-yay]

stamp: two stamps for England deux timbres pour l'Angleterre [duh tānbr poor lōngluh-tair]

station la gare [gar]

sticking plaster un pansement adhésif [pōns-mōn ahday-zeef]

stolen: my wallet's been stolen on m'a volé mon portefeuille [ōn mah voh-lay mōn pohrt-fuh-ee]

stop! arrêtez-vous! [ahray-tay-voo]

street une rue [roo]

strong fort [for]

student un étudiant [aytood-yōn]

sugar du sucre [sookr]

suitcase une valise [vah-leez]

sun le soleil [soh-lay]

sunburn un coup de soleil [koo duh soh-lay]

Sunday dimanche [dee-mōnsh]

sunglasses des lunettes de soleil [loo-net duh soh-lay]

sunshade un parasol

sunstroke une insolation [ānsoh-lahs-yōn]

suntan oil de l'huile solaire [weel soh-lair]

swim: I'm going for a swim je vais me baigner [juh vay muh bayn-yay]

table: a table for 4 une table pour quatre [oon tahbl poor kahtr]

taxi un taxi

tea le thé [tay]

telegram un télégramme [taylay-gram]

telephone le téléphone [taylay-fon]

UK is 19, wait for tone, then 44 and drop first 0 of area code

tent une tente [tōnt]

terrible affreux [ah-fruh]
thank you merci [mair-see]
   YOU MAY THEN HEAR
   de rien *you're welcome*
  no thank you non merci
that ce (cette) [suh, set]
  that one celui-là (celle-là) [suhlwee-lah, sel-lah]
  and that? et ça? [ay sah]
the le (la), (*plural*) les [luh, lah, lay]
them: with them avec eux (elles) [... uh, el]
there là [lah]
  is/are there ...? est-ce qu'il y a ...? [eskeel yah]
these: these apples ces pommes [say ...]
they ils (elles) [eel, el]
  are they ...? est-ce qu'ils (elles) sont ...? [ekeel (eskel) sōn]
thirsty: I'm thirsty j'ai soif [jay swahf]
this ce (cette) [suh, set]
  this one celui-ci (celle-ci) [suhlwee-see, sel-see]
  this is ... c'est [say]
  is this ...? est-ce que c'est ...? [eskuh say]
those: those people ces gens [say jōn]
Thursday jeudi [juh-dee]
ticket un billet [bee-yay]
time *see pages 124–125*
tired fatigué [fahtee-gay]
tissues des mouchoirs en papier [moo-shwahr ōn pahp-yay]
to: to London à Londres [ah lōndr]
  to England en Angleterre [ōn ōngluh-tair]
today aujourd'hui [ohjoor-dwee]
together ensemble [ōn-sōnbl]
toilet les toilettes [twah-let]
tomorrow demain [duh-mān]
  the day after tomorrow après-demain [ahpray-duh-mān]
tonight ce soir [suh swahr]
too trop [troh]; (*also*) aussi [oh-see]
  that's too much c'est trop [say ...]

....

tour une excursion [exkoors-yon]
tourist un touriste [too-reest]
towel une serviette [sairv-yet]
town une ville [veel]
train un train [trān]
translate traduire [trah-dweer]
travel agency une agence de voyage [ah-jons duh voh-yahj]
trousers un pantalon [pontah-lon]
try essayer [essay-yay]
Tuesday mardi [mahr-dee]
umbrella un parapluie [pahrah-plwee]
understand: I don't understand je ne comprends pas [juh nuh kon-pron pah]
urgent urgent [oor-jon]
us nous [noo]
use: can I use ...? est-ce que je peux utiliser ...? [eskuh juh puh ootee-lee-zay]
vegetarian végétarien [vayjay-tahr-yan]
very très [tray]
very much beaucoup [boh-koo]
village un village [vee-lahj]
wait: I'm waiting for ... j'attends ... [jah-ton]
wake: will you wake me up at 7.30? est-ce que vous pouvez me réveiller à 7.30? [eskuh voo poo-vay muh rayvay-yay ah set ur ay duh-mee]
Wales le Pays de Galles [payee duh gal]
want: I want ... je voudrais ... [juh voo-dray]
I don't want to je ne veux pas [juh nuh vuh pah]
warm chaud [shoh]
water l'eau [oh]
we nous [noo]
we are ... nous sommes ... [noo som]
Wednesday mercredi [mairkruh-dee]
week une semaine [suh-men]
well: how are you? – very well thanks comment allez-vous? – très bien, merci [koh-mont ah-lay voo – tray bee-yan mair-see]
wet mouillé [moo-yay]

....

what? quoi? [kwah]
  what is that? qu'est-ce que c'est?
  [keskuh say]
when? quand? [kōn]
where? où? [oo]
  where is ...? où est ...? [oo ay]
which? quel (quelle)? [kel]
  which one? lequel (laquelle)? [luh-kel ...]
white blanc [blōn]
who? qui? [kee]
why? pourquoi? [poor-kwah]
  why not? pourquoi pas?
wife: my wife ma femme [fam]
window la fenêtre [fuh-naitr]
wine du vin [vān]
with avec [ah-vek]
without sans [sōn]
woman une femme [fam]
work: it's not working ça ne marche pas [sah
  nuh marsh pah]
write: could you write it down? est-ce que vous
  pouvez me l'écrire? [eskuh voo poo-vay muh
  lay-kreer]
wrong faux [foh]
  what's wrong? qu'est-ce qu'il y a? [keskeel
  yah]
yacht un yacht [yot]
year une année [ah-nay]
yes oui [wee]
yesterday hier [yair]
you vous [voo]
  (*for people you know well*) tu [too]
  with you avec vous/toi [... twah]
  are you ...? est-ce que vous êtes/tu es ...? [eskuh
  vooz et, too ay]
young jeune [jurn]
your see **you** votre, (*plural*) vos [vohtr, voh];
  ton (ta), (*plural*) tes [tōn, toh, tay]
youth hostel une auberge de jeunesse [oh-bairj
  duh juh-ness]

0 zéro [zay-roh]

1 un [ān]	7 sept [set]
2 deux [duh]	8 huit [weet]
3 trois [trwah]	9 neuf [nurf]
4 quatre [kahtr]	10 dix [deess]
5 cinq [sānk]	11 onze [ōnz]
6 six [sees]	12 douze [dooz]

13 treize [trayz]	17 dix-sept [dee-set]
14 quatorze [kah-torz]	18 dix-huit [deez-weet]
15 quinze [kānz]	19 dix-neuf [deez-nurf]
16 seize [sayz]	20 vingt [vānt]

21 vingt-et-un [vān-tay-ān]
22 vingt-deux [vānt-duh]
23 vingt-trois [vānt-trwah]

30 trente [trōnt]	50 cinquante [sān-kōnt]
40 quarante [kah-rōnt]	60 soixante [swah-sōnt]

71 soixante-dix [swah-sōnt-deess]
71 soixante et onze [swah-sōnt ay ōnz]
72 soixante-douze [swah-sōnt dooz]
   in Switzerland and Belgium 'septante'
   [sep-tōnt] *'septante et un' etc*

80 quatre-vingts [kahtruh-vān]
81 quatre-vingt-un [... ān]
90 quatre-vingt-dix [kahtruh-vān-deess]
91 quatre-vingt-onze [... ōnz]
   in Switzerland and Belgium 'nonante'
   [nuh-nōnt] *'nonante et un' etc*

100 cent [sōn]
101 cent un [sōn ān]
200 deux cents
285 deux cent quatre-vingt-cinq
300 trois cents
400 quatre cents
1,000 mille [meel]
2,350 deux mille trois cent cinquante
1,000,000 un million [mee-yōn]

*for thousands use a full-stop or a space: 5.000 or
5 000; for decimals a comma: 4,6 [... veer-gool...]*

Entrées: Starters
Crudités *various salads and raw vegetables*
Cuisses de grenouille *frogs' legs*
Terrine du chef *pâté maison*
Oeufs mayonnaise *egg mayonnaise*
Bouchées à la reine *chicken vol-au-vent*

Potages: Soups
Crème de bolets *cream of mushroom*
Velouté de tomates *cream of tomato*
Soupe à l'oignon *onion soup*

Viandes: Meat dishes
Boeuf *beef*, porc *pork*, veau *veal*, agneau *lamb*
Rôti de boeuf *roast beef*
Gigot d'agneau *roast leg of lamb*
Côtelette de porc *pork chop*
Foie de veau *veal liver*
Langue de boeuf *tongue*
Bifteck *steak*
Tournedos *fillet steak*
Escalope panée *slice of veal in breadcrumbs*
Paupiettes de veau *veal olives*
Rognons madère *kidneys in madeira sauce*

Volaille: Poultry
Poule au riz *chicken and rice*
Poulet rôti *roast chicken*
Canard à l'orange *duck with orange*

Chasse: Game
Civet de lièvre *jugged hare*
Lapin chasseur *rabbit in white wine and herbs*

Poissons et marée: Fish and seafood
Coquilles Saint-Jacques *scallops*
Huîtres *oysters*
Moules marinière *mussels in white wine*
Truite aux amandes *trout with almonds*
Raie au beurre noir *skate in black butter*

Homard à l'armoricaine *lobster in white wine sauce with shallots*
Cabillaud *cod*, langouste *crayfish*, langoustine *scampi*, morue *salt cod*

A few menu terms:
à l'ail *(with) garlic*, aux câpres *in caper sauce*, à la crème *with cream*, garni *with chips (or rice) and vegetables*, en gelée *in aspic*, moutarde *with mustard*, provençale *cooked in olive oil with garlic, tomatoes and herbs*, au vin blanc *in white wine*, vinaigrette *with sharp vinegar dressing*

Légumes: Vegetables
Pommes de terre à l'anglaise *steamed potatoes*, pommes dauphine *potato croquettes*, (pommes) frites *chips*, purée *mashed potatoes*
Chou *cabbage*, chou-fleur *cauliflower*, courgettes *baby marrows*, épinards *spinach*, haricots verts *French beans*, petits pois *peas*

Salads
Salade *green salad with French dressing*
Salade niçoise *with green beans, peppers, anchovies, olives*
Salade russe *mixed vegetables in mayonnaise*

Dessert
Glace *ice cream*, flan *egg custard*
Tarte aux myrtilles *bilberry tart*
Cerises *cherries*, fraises *strawberries*, poire *pear*, pomme *apple*, pêche *peach*, raisin *grapes*

Snacks
Assiette anglaise *cold meats*, saucisse, frites *Frankfurter sausage and chips*, crêpes *pancakes*, croque-monsieur *toasted ham and cheese sandwich*, omelette au jambon/fromage *ham/cheese omelette*, sandwich aux rillettes *potted meat sandwich*

GERMAN

Special sounds in the pronunciation guide:

oo	is like oo in 'soon'
ꝏ	is like oo in 'book'
o̅o̅	is similar to the u sound in 'huge'
o̅w	is like the ow in 'cow'
k	is like the ch in Scottish 'loch'
uh	is pronounced as in 'a' or the u in 'butter'

Letters printed in italics show which part of a word should be stressed.

gute Reise!
[goo-tuh ry-zuh]
have a good trip!

....

a, an ein, eine, ein [ine, ine-uh, ine]
accident der Unfall [oonfal]
adaptor der Zwischenstecker [tsvishen-sht–]
address die Adresse [ad-ressuh]
after nach [nah*k*]
afternoon der Nachmittag [nah*k*-mi-tahg]
   good afternoon guten Tag! [goo-ten tahg]
again wieder [veeder]
airport der Flughafen [floog-hah-fen]
all alle [al-uh]
   all night/all day die ganze Nacht/den ganzen
   Tag [dee gants-uh nah*k*t/dayn gants-en tahg]
   all right! in Ordnung! [... ort-noong]
almost fast [fasst]
alone allein [al-*i*ne]
always immer
and und [oont]
another: another room ein anderes Zimmer
   [ine an-dress tsimmer]
   another beer noch ein Bier [no*k* ine beer]
arrive ankommen
ashtray ein Aschenbecher [ashen-besher]
ask fragen [frah-ghen]
baby ein Baby
back: I'll be right back ich bin gleich wieder da
   [ish bin glysh veeder dah]
bad schlecht [shlesht]
bag die Tasche [tash-uh]
bank die Bank
bar die Bar
bath das Bad [baht]
bathroom das Badezimmer [bah-duh-tsimmer]
beautiful schön [shurrn]
because weil [vile]
bed ein Bett
beer ein Bier [beer]
before vor [for]
best beste [best-uh]
better besser
bicycle ein Fahrrad [fahr-raht]

....

big groß [grohss]
bill die Rechnung [resh-noong]
black schwarz [shvarts]
blanket die Decke [deck-uh]
blue blau [blow]
boat das Boot [boht]
book das Buch [book]
boring langweilig [lang-vile-ish]
both beide [by-duh]
bottle die Flasche [flash-uh]
boy ein Junge [yoonguh]
brake die Bremse [brem-zuh]
bread das Brot [broht]
breakfast das Frühstück [froo-stöck]
broken kaputt
brother: my brother mein Bruder [mine brooder]
bus der Bus [booss]
bus stop die Bushaltestelle [booss-haltuh-shtelluh]
butter die Butter [booter]
café ein Café
camera die Kamera
campsite der Campingplatz
can: can I have ...? kann ich ... haben? [kan ish ... hah-ben]
  can you ...? können Sie ...? [kurrnen zee]
  I can't ... ich kann nicht ... [ish kan nisht]
cancel rückgängig machen [rook-geng-ish mahken]
car das Auto, der Wagen [ow-toh, vah-ghen]
car park ein Parkplatz
centre das Zentrum [tsen-troom]
change: can you change this into marks? könnten Sie das in Mark umtauschen? [kurrnten zee dass ... oom-tow-shen]
  I'd like to change my flight etc ich möchte umbuchen [ish murrshtuh oom-booken]
cheap billig [billish]
cheers! Prost [prohst]

....

cheese der Käse [kay-zuh]
chemist's die Drogerie [droh-guh-r*ee*]
cheque der Scheck [sheck]
children die Kinder [kin-der]
chips Pommes frites [pom frit]
church die Kirche [keer-shuh]
cigar eine Zigarre [tsig*a*rruh]
cigarette eine Zigarette [tsigarr-*e*ttuh]
clean sauber [z*o͞o*wber]
clothes die Kleidung [kly-d*oo*ng]
coat der Mantel
coffee ein Kaffee [kaffay]
   white coffee/black coffee Kaffee mit
   Milch/Kaffee schwarz [... mit milsh]
cold kalt
comb ein Kamm
come kommen; **come in** herein! [hair-rine]
constipation die Verstopfung [fair-sht*o*pf-*oo*ng]
consul der Konsul [kon-z*oo*l]
cost: what does it cost? was kostet das? [vass
   kostet dass]
could: could you please ...? könnten Sie bitte
   ...? [kurrnten zee bittuh ...]
   could I have ...? dürfte ich ... haben? [d*o͞o*rf-tuh
   ish ... hah-ben]
crazy verrückt [fair-r*o͞o*ckt]
crisps die Chips
Customs der Zoll [tsoll]
dark dunkel [d*oo*nkel]
daughter die Tochter [t*o*kter]
delicious köstlich [kurrst-lish]
dentist der Zahnarzt [tsahn-artst]
develop (*film*) entwickeln [ent-v--]
different: a different room ein anderes Zimmer
   [ine an-der-es ...]
difficult schwierig [shveerish]
dinner das (Abend)essen [ah-bent--]
do machen [mah*k*en]
   how do you do? guten Tag [gooten tahg]
   (*in the evening*) guten Abend [gooten ah-bent]

....

doctor der Arzt
door die Tür [töor]
dress das Kleid [klite]
drink: something to drink etwas zu trinken
 [etvass tsoo ...]
driving licence der Führerschein [föorer-shine]
drunk betrunken [buh-troonken]
dry-clean chemisch reinigen [shaymish
 ry-niggen]
early früh [fröo]
easy leicht [lysht]
eat: something to eat etwas zu essen
 [etvass tsoo ...]
else: something else etwas anderes [etvass ...]
England England [eng-glannt]
English englisch [eng-glish]
Englishman Engländer [eng-glender]
enough genug [gheh-noog]
entertainment die Unterhaltung
 [oonter-halt-oong]
evening der Abend [ah-bent]
 good evening guten Abend [gooten ...]
 this evening heute abend [hoytuh ...]
everyone jeder [yay-der]
everything alles [al-ess]
excellent ausgezeichnet [öwss-gheh-tsysh-net]
excuse: excuse me entschuldigen Sie!
 [ent-shool-dig-en zee]
expensive teuer [toy-er]
far: how far is it? wie weit ist es? [vee vite ...]
fast schnell
 don't speak so fast sprechen Sie nicht so
 schnell! [shpreshen zee nisht zoh ...]
father: my father mein Vater [mine fah-ter]
few: a few ein paar [ine pahr]
film der Film
first erste [air-stuh]
food das Essen
for für [föor]
fork die Gabel [gah-bel]

....

free frei [fry]
Friday Freitag [fry-tahg]
friend ein Freund [froynt]
from von [fon]
fun: it's fun das macht Spaß [... shpass]
funny (*strange, comical*) komisch [koh–]
garage (*repair*) eine Werkstatt [vairk-shtatt]
   (*petrol*) eine Tankstelle [–shtelluh]
   (*parking*) die Garage [ga-rah-djuh]
German deutsch [doytsh]
Germany Deutschland [doytsh-lannt]
girl ein Mädchen [mayt-shen]
give geben [gay-ben]
glasses die Brille [brill-uh]
go gehen [gay-en]; (*by vehicle*) fahren
   he's/it's gone er ist/es ist weg [air ist/ess ist
   vek]
good gut [goot]
goodbye auf Wiedersehen [ōwf vee-duh-zayn]
guide der Führer [fōoruh]
hairdresser's ein Friseur [free-zurr]
handbag die Handtasche [hannt-tash-uh]
happy glücklich [glōok-lish]
harbour der Hafen [hah-fen]
hard hart; (*difficult*) schwierig [shvee-rish]
have haben [hah-ben]
   I don't have time ich habe keine Zeit [ish
   hah-buh kine-uh tsite]
   do you have ...? haben Sie ...? [hah-ben zee ...]
he er [air]; **is he ...?** ist er ...?
headache Kopfschmerzen [–schmair-tsen]
hello hallo
help: can you help me? können Sie mir helfen?
   [kurrnen zee meer ...]
her sie [zee]; **with her** mit ihr [... eer]
   her bag ihre Tasche [ee-ruh tash-uh]
here hier [heer]
   come here komm her! [... hair]
him ihn [een]; **with him** mit ihm [... eem]
his sein [zine]

....

holiday der Feiertag [fy-er-tahg]
home: at home zu Hause [tsoo hōw-zuh]
hospital das Krankenhaus [–hōwss]
hot heiß [hice]
hotel das Hotel
hour eine Stunde [shtoon-duh]
house das Haus [hōwss]
how? wie? [vee]
   how many? wieviele? [vee-feel-uh]
   how much? wieviel? [vee-feel]
   how are you? wie geht's? [vee gayts]
hungry: I'm hungry/not hungry ich habe
   Hunger/ich habe keinen Hunger [ish hah-buh
   hoong-er/... kine-en ...]
hurt: it hurts es tut weh [ess toot vay]
husband: my husband mein Mann [mine ...]
I ich [ish]; **I am ...** ich bin ...
ice das Eis [ice]
ice cream ein Eis [ice]
if wenn [ven]
ill krank
immediately sofort [zohfort]
important wichtig [vish-tish]
in in
Ireland Irland [eer-lannt]
it es [ess]; **is it ...?** ist es ...?
jacket die Jacke [yack-uh]
just: just a little nur ein wenig [noor ine
   vayn-ish]
key der Schlüssel [shlōōss-el]
kiss der Kuß [kooss]
knife ein Messer
know: I don't know ich weiß nicht [ish vice
   nisht]
last letzte [lets-tuh]
   last night gestern abend; (*late*) gestern nacht
   [ghestern ah-bent/nah*k*t]
late spät [shpayt]
later später [shpayter]
   see you later! bis später! [biss ...]

leave: we're leaving tomorrow wir fahren morgen ab [veer fah-ren ... app]

when does the bus leave? wann fährt der Bus? [van fairt dair booss]

I left two shirts in my room ich habe zwei Hemden in meinem Zimmer liegenlassen [ish hah-buh tsvy ... lee-ghen-lassen]

can I leave this here? kann ich das hierlassen? [... heerlassen]

left: on the left links

left luggage die Gepäckaufbewahrung [gheh-peck-ōwf-buh-vahr-roong]

letter der Brief [breef]

light das Licht [lisht]

have you got a light? haben Sie Feuer? [hah-ben zee foy-er]

like: would you like ...? möchten Sie ...? [murrshten zee]

I'd like a .../I'd like to ... ich hätte gerne ein .../ich würde gerne ... [ish hett-uh gairn-uh ine/vōorduh ...]

I like it das gefällt mir [dass gheh-felt meer]

I don't like it das gefällt mir nicht [gheh-felt meer nisht]

little klein [kline]

a little ice ein wenig Eis [ine vay-nish ice]

a little more noch ein wenig [nok ...]

lorry der Lastwagen [lasst-vah-ghen]

lose: I've lost my ... ich habe mein ... verloren [ish hah-buh mine ... fair-lor-ren]

I'm lost ich habe mich verlaufen [ish hah-buh mish fair-lōwf-en]

lot: a lot/not a lot viel/nicht viel [feel]

luggage das Gepäck [gheh-peck]

lunch das Mittagessen [mittahg-essen]

main road die Hauptstraße [hōwpt-shtrahss-uh]

man der Mann

manager der Geschäftsführer [gheh-shefts-fōōr-er]

map eine Karte [kar-tuh]

market der Markt
match: a box of matches eine Schachtel
  Streichhölzer [shak-tel shtrysh-hurltser]
matter: it doesn't matter das macht nichts [dass
  mahkt nix]
maybe vielleicht [fee-lysht]
me mich [mish]; **with me** mit mir [... meer]
mean: what does that mean? was heißt das?
  [vass hysst dass]
menu die Speisekarte [shpy-zuh-kar-tuh]
milk die Milch [milsh]
mine mein [mine]
mineral water ein Mineralwasser
  [minerahl-vasser]
minute die Minute [minoo-tuh]
Monday Montag [mohntahg]
money das Geld [gelt]
more mehr [mair]
  more wine, please noch etwas Wein, bitte
  [nok etvass vine bittuh]
morning der Morgen [mor-ghen]
  good morning guten Morgen [gooten ...]
mother die Mutter [mooter]
motorbike das Motorrad [moh-tor-raht]
motorway die Autobahn [ōwtoh-bahn]
mountain der Berg [bairk]
much viel [feel]
  not much nicht viel [nisht feel]
music die Musik [moozeek]
must: I must ... ich muß ... [ish mooss]
  I must not eat ... ich darf ... nicht essen [ish
  darf ... nisht ...]
  you must Sie müssen [zee moossen]
my mein [mine]
name der Name [nah-muh]
  my name is ... ich heiße ... [ish hyss-uh ...]
  what's your name? wie heißen Sie? [vee
  hyssen zee]
near in der Nähe [in dair nay-uh]
necessary notwendig [noht-vendish]

....

needle die Nadel [nah-del]
never niemals [nee-mallts]
new neu [noy]
newspaper eine Zeitung [tsytoong]
next nächster [nexter]
nice schön [shurrn]; (person) nett
night die Nacht [nah*k*t]
   good night gute Nacht [gootuh nah*k*t]
no nein [nine]
   no water kein Wasser [kine vasser]
nobody niemand [nee-mannt]
noisy laut [lōwt]
not nicht [nisht]
   not that one das nicht [dass nisht]
   not me ich nicht
   I don't smoke ich rauche nicht [ish rōw*k*uh nisht]
nothing nichts [nix]
now jetzt [yetst]
nowhere nirgends [neer-ghents]
number die Zahl [tsahl]
of von [fon]
often oft
oil das Öl [urrl]
OK okay
old alt
on auf [ōwf]
one ein [ine]
only nur [noor]
open offen; (shop etc) geöffnet [gheh-urrf-net]
or oder [oh-der]
orange juice der Orangensaft [oronjen-zafft]
other: the other one der (die, das) andere [dair (dee, dass) an-der-uh]
our unser [oon-zer]
over: over there/here dort/hier drüben [dort/heer drōōben]
pain der Schmerz [shmairts]
painkillers schmerzstillende Mittel [shmairts-shtill-end-uh ...]

paper das Papier [pa-p*eer*]
pardon? wie bitte? [vee bittuh]
passport der Paß [pas]
pen der Kugelschreiber [kooghel-shryber]
people die Leute [loy-tuh]
petrol das Benzin [ben-ts*een*]
photograph eine Fotografie [foto-gra-f*ee*]
piece das Stück [sht**oo**ck]
plane das Flugzeug [floog-tsoyg]
platform: which platform? welches Gleis?
   [velshes glice]
please bitte [bittuh]
police die Polizei [polits-*eye*]
pool das Schwimmbad [shvimm-baht]
possible möglich [murr-glish]
postcard die Postkarte [posst-kar-tuh]
post office das Postamt [posst-amt]
pretty hübsch [h**oo**psh]
problem das Problem [prob-l*ay*m]
pronounce: how do you pronounce it? wie
   spricht man das aus? [vee shprisht ... **ow**ss]
purse das Portemonnaie [port-mon-*ay*]
quiet ruhig [roo-ish]; (*not noisy*) still [shtill]
quite ganz [gants]
rain: it's raining es regnet [ess rayg-net]
ready: when will it be ready? wann ist es
   fertig? [van ist ess fair-tish]
receipt eine Quittung [kvit-**oo**ng]
red rot [roht]
rent: can I rent a car/bike? kann ich ein
   Auto/Fahrrad mieten? [... meeten]
repair: can you repair it? können Sie es
   reparieren? [kurrnen zee ess rep-a-r*ee*-ren]
reservation die Reservierung [rez-air-v*ee*-r**oo**ng]
restaurant ein Restaurant [–rong]
return: a return to ... eine Rückfahrkarte
   nach ... [ine-uh r**oo**ck-far-kar-tuh nah*k*]
right: on the right rechts [reshts]
   that's right das stimmt [dass shtimmt]
river der Fluß [fl**oo**ss]

....

road die Straße [shtrass-uh]
room das Zimmer [tsimmer]
  a (single/double) room ein (Einzel/Doppel)
  zimmer [ine (ine-tsel/doppel) ...]
  for one night/for three nights für eine
  Nacht/für drei Nächte [foor ine-uh nahkt/foor
  dry neshte]
safe sicher [zisher]
salt das Salz [zalts]
same der-/die-/dasselbe [dair-/dee-/dass-zelbuh]
  the same again das gleiche noch mal [dass
  glysh-uh nok mal]
Saturday Samstag [zamz-tahg]
say: how do you say ... in German? was heißt ...
  auf Deutsch? [vass hysst ... owf doytsh]
  what did he say? was hat er gesagt? [vass hat
  air gheh-zahgt]
scissors eine Schere [ine-uh shay-ruh]
Scotland Schottland [shot-lannt]
sea das Meer [mayr]
seat der (Sitz)platz
see sehen [zay-en]
  can I see the room? kann ich mir das Zimmer
  anschauen? [kan ish meer dass tsimmer
  an-show-en]
  oh, I see ach so! [ahk zoh]
send schicken [shicken]
shampoo ein Shampoo(n)
she sie [zee]; **is she ...?** ist sie ...?
shirt das Hemd [hemmt]
shoes die Schuhe [shoo-uh]
shop das Geschäft [gheh-shefft]
show: please show me bitte zeigen Sie es mir
  [bittuh tsy-ghen zee ess meer]
shower: with shower mit Dusche [mit doosh-uh]
shut zu [tsoo]
single: a single to ... einmal einfach nach ...
  [ine-mal ine-fahk nahk]
sister: my sister meine Schwester [mine-uh
  shvester]

sit: can I sit here? kann ich mich hierher setzen?
[kan ish mish heer-hair zetsen]
skirt der Rock
slow langsam [*lang*-zahm]
small klein [kline]
so so [zoh]
   not so much nicht so viel [nisht zoh feel]
soap die Seife [zy-fuh]
somebody jemand [yay-mannt]
something etwas [etvass]
son: my son mein Sohn [mine zohn]
soon bald [balt]
sorry: (I'm) sorry Entschuldigung!
[ent-shool-digoong]
souvenir ein Souvenir
speak: do you speak English? sprechen Sie
Englisch? [shpreshen zee eng-glish]
   I don't speak ... ich kann kein ... [ish kan kine]
spoon der Löffel [lurr-fel]
stairs die Treppe [trep-uh]
stamp eine Briefmarke [breef-mark-uh]
   two stamps for England zwei Briefmarken
für England [tsvy ... foor eng-glannt]
station der Bahnhof [bahn-hohff]
sticking plaster ein (Heft)pflaster
stolen: my wallet's been stolen man hat mir
meine Brieftasche gestohlen [man hat meer
mine-uh breef-tash-uh gheh-shtole-en]
stop! halt! [hallt]
street die Straße [shtrahss-uh]
strong stark [shtark]
student der Student [shtoo-dent]
sugar der Zucker [tsoocker]
suitcase der Koffer
sun die Sonne [zonnuh]
Sunday Sonntag [zonn-tahg]
swim: I'm going for a swim ich gehe
schwimmen [ish gay-uh shvimmen]
table: a table for 4 ein Tisch für vier [ine tish foor
feer]

....

taxi ein Taxi
tea der Tee [tay]
telegram ein Telegramm
telephone das Telefon
   UK is 0044 and drop first 0 of area code
tent das Zelt [tselt]
terrible schrecklich [shrecklish]
thank you danke(schön) [dank-uh(shurrn)]
  YOU MAY THEN HEAR
  bitteschön, bitte sehr *you're welcome*
  no thank you nein danke [nine ...]
that: that man dieser Mann (da) [deez-er ...]
  that one das da
the der, die, das; *(plural)* die
them sie [zee]; **with them** mit ihnen [... een-en]
there dort
  is there/are there ...? gibt es ...? [gheept ess ...]
these diese [deez-uh]
they sie [zee]; **are they ...?** sind sie ...? [zinnt ...]
thirsty: I'm thirsty ich habe Durst [ish hah-buh
  doorst]
this dieser [deez-er]
  this one dieser hier [... heer]
  is this ...? ist das ...?
those diese (da) [deez-uh (dah)]
Thursday Donnerstag [donners-tahg]
ticket die Fahrkarte [–kar-tuh]
  (plane) das Ticket
time die Zeit [tsite]; *see pages 124-125*
tired müde [moo-duh]
tissues Papiertaschentücher
  [pa-peer-tashen-took-er]
to: to England/Berlin nach England/Berlin
  [nahk ...]
today heute [hoy-tuh]
together zusammen [tsoo-zammen]
toilet die Toilette [twa-lettuh]
tomorrow morgen [mor-ghen]
  the day after tomorrow übermorgen
  [oober–]

....

tonight heute abend [hoy-tuh ah-bent]
too zu [tsoo]; (also) auch [ōwk]
  too much zuviel [tsoo-feel]
tourist der Tourist
tourist office das Fremdenverkehrsbüro
  [frem-den-fair-kairs-bōō-roh]
towel das Handtuch [hant-took]
town die Stadt [shtat]
train der Zug [tsoog]
tram die Straßenbahn [shtrahssen-bahn]
translate übersetzen [ōōber-zet-sen]
travel agency das Reisebüro [ry-zuh-bōō-roh]
trousers die Hose [hoh-zuh]
try versuchen [fair-zook-en]
Tuesday Dienstag [deenz-tahg]
twice zweimal [tsvy-mal]
umbrella der Schirm [sheerm]
understand: I don't understand das verstehe
  ich nicht [dass fair-shtay-uh ish nisht]
urgent dringend [dring-ent]
us uns [ōonts]
use: can I use ...? kann ich ... benutzen? [kan ish
  buh-nōot-sen]
vegetarian ein Vegetarier [vay-gheh-tar-ee-er]
very sehr [zair]
village das Dorf
wait: I'm waiting for a friend ich warte auf
  einen Freund [ish var-tuh ōwf ine-en froynt]
wake: will you wake me up at 7.30? wecken Sie
  mich bitte um 7.30 [vecken zee mish bittuh ōom
  halp ahkt]
Wales Wales [vayls]
want: I want a ... ich möchte ein ... [ish
  murrshtuh ine]
  I don't want to ich will nicht [ish vill nisht]
warm warm [varm]
water das Wasser [vasser]
we wir [veer]; **we are ...** wir sind ... [veer zinnt]
Wednesday Mittwoch [mit-vok]
week die Woche [vock-uh]

....

well: how are you? – very well, thanks wie
geht's? – danke, gut! [vee gayts dankuh goot]
wet naß [nass]
what? was? [vass]
when? wann? [van]
where? wo? [voh]
   where is ...? wo ist ...?
which? welcher? [velsher]
white weiß [vice]
who? wer? [vair]
why? warum? [varoom]
   why not? warum nicht? [... nisht]
wife: my wife meine Frau [mine-uh frōw]
window das Fenster
wine der Wein [vine]
with mit
without ohne [oh-nuh]
woman die Frau [frōw]
work: it's not working es funktioniert nicht [ess
foonk-tsee-oh-neert nisht]
write schreiben [shryben]
   could you write it down, please? könnten Sie
das bitte aufschreiben? [kurrnten zee dass
bittuh ōwf-shryben]
wrong falsch [falsh]
   there's something wrong with ... da stimmt
etwas nicht mit ... [... etvass ...]
   what's wrong? was ist los? [vass ist lohss]
year das Jahr [y–]
yes ja [yah]
yesterday gestern [ghestern]
you Sie [zee]
   (for people you know well) du [doo]
   are you ...? sind Sie/bist du ...? [zinnt zee]
   for you für Sie/dich [foor .../dish]
   with you mit Ihnen/dir [... een-en/deer]
young jung [yoong]
your Ihr [eer]/dein [dine]
youth hostel die Jugendherberge
[yoo-ghent-hair-bair-guh]

0 null [nōōl]

1 eins [ine-ts]	17 siebzehn [zeep–]
2 zwei [tsvy]	18 achtzehn
3 drei [dry]	19 neunzehn
4 vier [feer]	20 zwanzig [tsvan-tsi*k*]
5 fünf [fōōnf]	21 einundzwanzig
6 sechs [zex]	[ine-ɔɔnt–]
7 sieben [zeeben]	22 zweiundzwanzig
8 acht [ah*k*t]	23 dreiundzwanzig
9 neun [noyn]	24 vierundzwanzig
10 zehn [tsayn]	25 fünfundzwanzig
11 elf	26 sechsundzwanzig
12 zwölf [tsvurrlf]	27 siebenundzwanzig
13 dreizehn [dry-tsayn]	28 achtundzwanzig
14 vierzehn	29 neunundzwanzig
15 fünfzehn	30 dreißig [dry-tsi*k*]
16 sechzehn	

31 einunddreißig	60 sechzig
32 zweiunddreißig	70 siebzig [zeep–]
40 vierzig [feer-tsi*k*]	80 achtzig
50 fünfzig	90 neunzig

100 hundert [hɔɔndert]
101 hunderteins
175 hundertfünfundsiebzig
 [hɔɔndert-fōōnf-ɔɔnt-zeep-tsi*k*]
200 zweihundert
300 dreihundert
400 vierhundert
500 fünfhundert
600 sechshundert
700 siebenhundert
800 achthundert
900 neunhundert
1,000 tausend [tōw-zent]
2,000 zweitausend
4,653 viertausendsechshundertdreiundfünfzig
1,000,000 eine Million [ine-uh mil-ee-yone]

for thousands use a full-stop: 6.000
for decimals use a comma: 4,6 [... Komma ...]

....

Vorspeisen: Hors d'oeuvre
Geräucherter Aal *smoked eel*
Königinpastetchen *chicken vol-au-vent*
Krabbencocktail *prawn cocktail*
Weinbergschnecken *snails*

Suppen: Soups
Blumenkohlsuppe *cream of cauliflower*
Flädlesuppe *(Swabia) consommé with pancake strips*
Gulaschsuppe *goulash soup*
Hühnerbrühe *chicken broth*
Klößchensuppe *clear soup with dumplings*
Kraftbrühe mit Ei *consommé with a raw egg*
Ochsenschwanzsuppe *oxtail soup*
Tagessuppe *soup of the day*

Vom Rind: Beef
Bouletten *(Berlin) meat balls*
Deutsches Beefsteak *mince patty*
Rinderbraten *pot roast*
Rinderfilet *fillet steak*
Rindsrouladen *beef olives*
Rostbraten *(Swabia) steak with onions*
Sauerbraten *marinaded potroast beef*

Vom Schwein: Pork
Eisbein *knuckles of pork*
Karbonade *(Berlin) roast ribs of pork*
Kotelett *chops*
Leberkäse *(South Ger) baked pork and beef loaf*
Schweinebraten *roast pork*
Schweineschnitzel *pork fillets*

Vom Kalb: Veal
Gefüllte Kalbsbrust *veal roll*
Kalbshaxe *leg of veal*
Jägerschnitzel *veal with mushrooms*
Wiener Schnitzel *veal in breadcrumbs*
Zigeunerschnitzel *veal with peppers and relishes*

Wild: Game
Rehbraten *roast venison*
Wildschweinsteak *wild boar steak*

Fischgerichte: Fish
Forelle Müllerin *trout with butter and lemon*
Hecht *pike*
Karpfen blau *boiled blue carp*
Matjesheringe *pickled herrings*

Others
Bockwurst *large Frankfurter sausage*
Bratwurst *grilled pork sausage*
Halbes Hähnchen *half a (roast) chicken*

Spezialitäten: Specialities
Himmel und Erde *(Rhineland) potatoes and apple
    sauce with black pudding*
Labskaus *(Hamburg) potatoes mixed with pieces
    of fish and meat*
Weißwürste mit Senf *(Munich) white sausages
    and sweet mustard*

Beilagen: Side dishes
Blumenkohl *cauliflower*; Bratkartoffeln *roast
    potatoes*; Erbsen *peas*; gemischter Salat *mixed
    salad*; Gemüseplatte *mixed veg*; Kartoffelpüree
    mashed potatoes; Klöße, Knödel *dumplings*;
    Pommes Frites *French fried potatoes*;
    Rosenkohl *Brussel sprouts*; Salzkartoffeln
    boiled potatoes; Sauerkraut *finely chopped
    pickled cabbage*; Spargel *asparagus*; Spätzle
    homemade noodles

Nachspeisen: Desserts
Gemischtes Eis mit Sahne *assorted ice creams
    with whipped cream*
Eisbecher *knickerbocker glory*
Obstsalat *fruit salad*
Rote Grütze *(North Germany) fruit blancmange*

SPANISH

Special sound in the pronunciation guide:

h   is like the ch in Scottish 'loch'

Letters printed in italics show which part of a word should be stressed.

¡buen viaje!
[bwem bee-*ah*eh]
have a good trip!

....

a, an un; una [oon, *oo*na]
accident un accidente [aktheed*e*nteh]
adaptor un adaptador
address la dirección [deerekth-yon]
after después [dess-pwess]
afternoon la tarde [t*a*r-deh]
  good afternoon buenas tardes [bweh-nass t*a*rdess]
again otra vez [*o*h-tra veth]
airport el aeropuerto [ah-airoh-pw*ai*r-toh]
all todo [t*o*h-doh]
  all night toda la noche [t*o*h-da la n*o*tcheh]
almost casi [k*a*h-see]
alone solo
always siempre [see-*e*m-preh]
and y [ee]
another otro
arrive llegar [yeh-g*a*r]
ashtray un cenicero [thenee-th*e*h-roh]
ask preguntar
  could you ask him to ...? ¿podría pedirle que ...? [pod-r*ee*-a ped*ee*r-leh keh]
baby un bebé [beh-beh]
back: I'll be back soon estaré de vuelta pronto [esstareh deh vwelta ...]
bad malo
bag una bolsa; (*handbag, suitcase*) un bolso
bank el banco
bar el bar
bath un baño [b*a*hn-yoh]
bathroom cuarto de baño [kw*a*rtoh deh b*a*hn-yoh]
beach la playa [pl*a*-ya]
beautiful precioso [preth-y*o*h-soh]
because porque [p*o*r-keh]
bed una cama
beer cerveza [thairveh-tha]
before antes [*a*n-tess]
best el mejor [m*e*hor]
better mejor [m*e*hor]

bicycle una bicicleta [beethee-kleh-ta]
big grande [gran-deh]
bill la cuenta [kwenta]
black negro [neh-groh]
blanket una manta
blue azul [athool]
boat un barco
book un libro [lee–]
boring aburrido [abooreedoh]
both los dos
bottle una botella [boteh-ya]
boy un chico [cheekoh]
brake el freno [freh-noh]
bread pan
breakfast el desayuno [dessa-yoonoh]
broken roto
brother: my brother mi hermano [mee
air-mah-noh]
brown marrón; (*tanned*) moreno [moreh-noh]
bull el toro
bull fight una corrida de toros [korree-da deh ...]
bus un autobús [ow-toh-booss]
bus stop la parada del autobús
butter mantequilla [mantekeeya]
café una cafetería [kafeh-teh-ree-a]
camera una máquina de fotos [makeena ...]
campsite un camping
can: can I have ...? ¿me da ...? [meh da]
  can you ...? ¿podría ...? [pod-ree-a]
  I can't ... no puedo ... [noh pweh-doh]
cancel anular
car un coche [koh-cheh]
car park un aparcamiento [–mee-entoh]
centre el centro [th–]
change: can you change this into pesetas?
  ¿puede cambiarme esto en pesetas? [pweh-deh
  kam-bee-ar-meh ...]
  I want to change my reservation quisiera
  cambiar mi reserva [kees-yeh-ra kam-bee-ar
  mee ...]

....

cheap barato
cheers! salud [saloo]
cheese queso [keh-soh]
chemist's una farmacia [far-math-ya]
cheque un cheque [cheh-keh]
children los niños [neen-yoss]
chips patatas fritas [pa-tah-tass freetass]
church una iglesia [ee-gleh-see-a]
cigar un puro [poo-roh]
cigarette un cigarillo [theegaree-yo]
clean limpio [leemp-yo]
clothes la ropa
coat un abrigo [–bree–]
coffee un café [kaffeh]
   white coffee/black coffee café con leche/café
   solo [... kon leh-cheh ...]
cold frío [free-oh]
comb un peine [pay-neh]
come venir [veneer]
   come on! ¡vamos! [bah-moss]
constipation estreñimiento
   [esstren-yeem-yentoh]
consul el cónsul
cost: what does it cost? ¿cuánto cuesta?
   [kwantoh kwesssta]
could: could you please ...? ¿podría usted ...?
   [podree-a oosteh ...]
   could I have ...? quiero ... [kee-eh-roh]
crazy loco
crisps patatas fritas a la inglesa [freetass]
Customs la aduana [ad-wah-na]
dark oscuro [–koo–]
daughter: my daughter mi hija [mee ee-ha]
delicious delicioso [deleeth-yosoh]
dentist un dentista
develop: could you develop these? ¿podría
   revelármelas? [podree-a reh-velar-meh-lass]
different: they are different son diferentes
difficult difícil [deefeetheel]
dinner la cena [theh-na]

do hacer [ath*ai*r]
  how do you do? hola, ¿qué tal? [*o*h-la keh ...]
doctor el médico
door una puerta [pw*ai*r-ta]
dress un vestido [–t*ee*doh]
drink: something to drink algo de beber [... deh
  beb*ai*r]
driving licence el permiso de conducir
  [pair-m*ee*-soh deh kondoo-th*ee*r]
drunk bor*r*acho
dry-clean limpiar en seco [leemp-y*ar* ...]
early tempr*a*no
easy fácil [f*a*h-theel]
eat: something to eat algo de comer [... deh
  koh-m*ai*r]
else: something else algo más
England Inglaterra
English inglés [eengl*e*ss]
enough suficiente [soo-feeth-y*e*nteh]
entertainment diversiones [deevairs-y*o*h-ness]
evening la tarde [t*ar*-deh]
  good evening buenas tardes [bw*e*h-nass
  t*ar*dess]
everyone todos
everything todo
excellent excelente [ess-thell*e*nteh]
excuse me (*to get past etc*) con permiso
  [... pair-m*ee*-soh]
  (*to get attention*) ¡por favor!
  (*apology*) perdone [pair-d*o*h-neh]
expensive caro
far: how far is it? ¿a qué distancia está? [ah keh
  dee-st*a*nth-ya ...]
fast rápido
  don't speak so fast no hable tan de prisa [noh
  *a*h-bleh tan deh pr*ee*-sa]
father: my father mi padre [mee p*a*h-dreh]
ferry el ferry
few: a few days unos días [... d*ee*–]
film una película [peh-l*ee*-koola]

....

first el primero [pree-meh-roh]
fish un pez [peth]; (*food*) pescado
food comida [kommeeda]
for para
fork un tenedor
free libre [lee-breh]
Friday viernes [vee-air-ness]
friend un amigo [amee-goh]
from de [deh]
fun: it's fun es divertido [deev-air-teedoh]
funny (*strange*) raro
    (*comical*) gracioso [grath-yoh-soh]
garage (*repair*) un taller [ta-yair]
    (*petrol*) una gasolinera [–eeneh-ra]
girl una chica [chee-ka]
give dar
glasses las gafas
go ir [eer]
    he's gone se ha ido [seh ...]
good bueno [bweh-noh]
goodbye adiós
guide un guía [ghee-a]
guitar una guitarra [gheetarra]
hairdresser's una peluquería [pelookeh-ree-ah]
handbag un bolso
happy contento
harbour el puerto [pwair-toh]
hard duro [doo–]
    (*difficult*) difícil [deefeetheel]
have: do you have ...? ¿tiene usted ...?
    [tee-eh-neh oosteh ...]
    I don't have ... no tengo ...
he él; **is he ...?** ¿es ...?
headache dolor de cabeza [... deh kabeh-tha]
hello ¡hola! [o-la]
help ayuda [–yoo–]
    can you help me? ¿puede ayudarme?
    [pweh-deh ah-yoo-dar-meh]
her: with her con ella [... eh-ya]
    her bag su bolso

....

here aquí [ak*ee*]
him: for him para él
his: his drink su bebida
holiday vacaciones [vacath-y*oness*]
home: at home en casa [... k*ah*-sa]
hospital el hospital [osspeet*a*l]
hot caliente [kal-y*e*nteh]
hotel un hotel [oh-t*e*l]
hour una hora [*ora*]
house una casa [k*ah*-sa]
how? ¿cómo?
  how many? ¿cuántos? [kw–]
  how much? ¿cuánto?
  how long does it take? ¿cuánto se tarda?
  [... seh ...]
  how are you? ¿cómo está usted? [... *oo*steh]
hungry: I'm hungry/not hungry tengo/no tengo
  hambre [... *a*mbreh]
hurt: it hurts me duele [m*e*h dw*e*h-leh]
husband: my husband mi marido [mee
  mar*ee*doh]
I yo; **I am ...** soy ...
ice hielo [y*e*h-loh]
ice cream un helado [eh-l*a*h-doh]
if si [see]
ill enfermo [–f*air*–]
immediately ahora mismo [ah-*o*ra m*ee*zmoh]
important importante [–teh]
in en
Ireland Irlanda [eer–]
it: is it ...? ¿es ...?
jacket una chaqueta [chack*e*h-ta]
just: just a little sólo un poquito [... pok*ee*toh]
key la llave [y*ah*-veh]
kiss un beso [b*e*h-soh]
knife un cuchillo [kooch*ee*-yoh]
know: I don't know no sé [noh seh]
last último [*oo*l–]
  last night anoche [an*o*tcheh]
late tarde [t*a*r-deh]

....

later más tarde
  see you later hasta luego [asta lweh-goh]
leave: we're leaving tomorrow nos vamos
  mañana [noss vah-moss man-yah-na]
  when does the bus leave? ¿a qué hora sale el
  autobús? [ah keh ora sah-leh el ow-toh-booss]
  I left two shirts in my room me dejé dos
  camisas en mi habitación [meh deheh doss
  kamee-sass en mee abbee-tath-yon]
  can I leave this here? ¿puedo dejar esto aquí?
  [pweh-doh dehar estoh akee]
left: on the left a la izquierda [eeth-kee-air-da]
left luggage (office) la consigna de equipajes
  [konseegna deh ekeepah-hess]
letter una carta
light la luz [looth]
  have you got a light? ¿tiene fuego?
  [tee-eh-neh fweh-goh]
like: would you like ...? ¿quiere usted ...?
  [kee-eh-reh oosteh]
  I'd like a .../I'd like to ... quisiera un
  .../quisiera ... [kees-yeh-ra]
  I like it/you me gusta/gustas [goo–]
  I don't like it no me gusta
little pequeño [peckehn-yoh]
  a little ice/a little more un poco de hielo/un
  poco más [... yeh-loh ...]
  only a little sólo un poquito [poh-kee-toh]
lorry un camión [kam-yon]
lose: I've lost my ... he perdido mi ... [eh
  pairdeedoh mee]
  I'm lost me he perdido
lot: a lot/not a lot mucho/no mucho [moo-choh]
luggage equipaje [eckee-pah-heh]
lunch el almuerzo [al-mwair-thoh]
main road una calle principal [ka-yeh
  preentheepal]
  (*in the country*) la carretera principal
man un hombre [ombreh]
manager el director [dee–]

map un mapa
market un mercado [mair–]
match: a box of matches una caja de cerillas
  [kah-ha deh theree-yass]
matter: it doesn't matter no importa
maybe tal vez [... veth]
me: for me para mí [... mee]
mean: what does that mean? ¿qué significa
  esto? [keh signifeeka ...]
menu el menú [menoo]
milk leche [leh-cheh]
mineral water agua mineral [ahg-wa
  meeneh-ral]
minute un minuto [–eenoo–]
Monday lunes [looness]
money dinero [dee-neh-roh]
more más
  more wine, please más vino, por favor
morning la mañana [man-yah-na]
  good morning buenos días [bweh-noss dee-ass]
mother: my mother mi madre [mee mah-dreh]
motorbike una moto
motorway autopista [ow-topeesta]
mountain una montaña [montahn-ya]
much mucho [mootchoh]
  not much no mucho
music música [moosseeka]
must: I must ... tengo que ... [... keh]
  I must not eat ... no debo comer ... [noh deh-boh
  komair]
  you must (do it) debe usted de hacerlo [deh-beh
  oosteh deh athair-loh]
my mi [mee]
name el nombre [–breh]
  my name is ... me llamo ... [meh yah-moh]
  what's your name? ¿cómo se llama usted?
  [... seh yah-ma oosteh]
near: is it near? ¿está cerca? [... thair-ka]
  near here cerca de aquí [... deh akee]
necessary necesario [nethessar-yoh]

....

needle una aguja [ag*oo-h*a]
never nunca
new nuevo [nw*eh*-voh]
newspaper un periódico
next próximo
nice agradable [–d*a*h-bleh]
night noche [n*o*tcheh]
   good night buenas noches [bw*eh*-nass
   n*o*tchess]
no no
   there's no water no hay agua [noh eye *a*hgwa]
nobody nadie [n*a*hd-yeh]
noisy ruidoso [rweed*o*soh]
not no
   not me yo no
   not that one ese no [*eh*-seh ...]
nothing nada
now ahora [ah-*o*ra]
nowhere en ningún sitio [en neeng*oo*n s*ee*t-yoh]
number un número [n*oo*–]
of de [deh]
often a menudo [ah men*oo*doh]
oil aceite [ath*a*y-teh]
OK! ¡vale! [b*a*h-leh]
old viejo [vee-eh-*h*oh]
on en
one uno [*oo*no]
only: only one sólo uno
open abierto [ab-y*a*irtoh]
or o
orange juice zumo de naranja [th*oo*-moh deh
   nar*a*n-ha]
other: the other one el *o*tro
our nuestro [nw*e*sstroh]
over: over here/there aquí/allá [ak*ee*/a-ya]
pain dolor
painkillers calmantes [kalm*a*ntess]
paper papel
pardon? ¿cómo?
passport pasaporte [passap*o*rteh]

pen una pluma [plooma]
people gente [henteh]
petrol gasolina [–eena]
photograph una foto
piece un pedazo [pedah-thoh]
plane un avión [av-yon]
platform: **which platform, please?** ¿qué andén,
  por favor? [keh ...]
please por favor [... fa-vor]
police la policía [–thee-a]
pool (swimming) una piscina [peess-theena]
possible posible [posseebleh]
postcard una postal
post office la oficina de Correos [offee-theena ...]
pretty mono
problem un problema
pronounce: **how do you pronounce this?**
  ¿cómo se pronuncia esto? [... pronoonth-ya ...]
purse el monedero
quiet tranquilo [–keeloh]
quite (fairly) bastante [–teh]
rain: **it's raining** está lloviendo [... yov-yendoh]
ready: **when will it be ready?** ¿cuándo estará
  listo? [kwandoh estara leestoh]
receipt un recibo [rethee-boh]
red rojo [roh-hoh]
rent: **can I rent a car/bicycle?** ¿puedo alquilar
  un coche/una bicicleta? [pweh-doh alkeelar oon
  kotcheh/beetheekleh-ta]
repair: **can you repair it?** ¿puede arreglarlo?
  [pweh-deh ...]
reservation una reserva [–sair–]
restaurant un restaurante [rest-ow-ranteh]
return: **a return/two returns to ...** un billete/dos
  billetes de ida y vuelta a ... [... beeyeh-teh ... deh
  eeda ee vwelta]
right: **on the right** a la derecha
  that's right eso es
river un río [ree-oh]
road la carretera

....

room la habitación [abee-tath-yon]
   a single/double room una habitación
   individual/doble [... eendeeveed-wal/dobleh]
   for one night/for three nights para una
   noche/para tres noches [... notcheh ...]
safe seguro [–goo–]
salt sal
same mismo [meez-moh]
   the same again, please lo mismo otra vez, por
   favor [... veth ...]
Saturday sábado
say: how do you say ... in Spanish? ¿cómo se
   dice ... en español? [... seh dee-theh ...]
   what did he say? ¿qué ha dicho? [keh ah
   deechoh]
scissors unas tijeras [tee-heh-rass]
Scotland Escocia [eskoth-ya]
sea el mar
seat el asiento [assee-entoh]
see: can I see the room? ¿puedo ver la
   habitación? [pweh-doh vair la abbee-tath-yon]
   oh, I see ah, ya comprendo
send enviar [embee-ar]
shampoo el champú [champoo]
she ella [eh-ya]; **is she ...?** ¿es ...?
shirt una camisa [kamee-sa]
shoes zapatos [tha–]
shop una tienda [tee-enda]
show: please show me por favor, enséñeme
   [... ensen-yeh-meh]
shower: with shower con ducha [dootcha]
shut cerrado [therrah-doh]
single: a single to ... un billete para ...
   [... beel-yeh-teh ...]
sister: my sister mi hermana [mee air-mah-na]
sit: can I sit here? ¿puedo sentarme aquí?
   [pweh-doh sentarmeh akee]
skirt una falda
slow lento
small pequeño [peckehn-yoh]

so: it's so hot hace tanto calor [*ah*-theh ...]
   not so much no tanto
soap jabón [*h*abon]
somebody alguien [*a*lg-yen]
something algo
son: my son mi hijo [mee *ee-h*oh]
soon pronto
sorry: (I'm) sorry ¡perdón! [pair-don]
souvenir un recuerdo [rekw*ai*r-doh]
Spain España [esp*a*n-ya]
Spanish español [espan-y*o*l]
   I don't speak Spanish no hablo español [noh *a*h-bloh ...]
speak: do you speak English? ¿habla inglés? [*a*h-bla eengl*e*ss]
   I don't speak ... no hablo ... [noh *a*h-bloh]
spoon una cuchara [koo–]
stairs la escalera
stamp un sello [s*e*h-yoh]
   two stamps for England dos sellos para Inglaterra
station la estación [esstath-yon]
sticking plaster una tirita [teer*ee*ta]
stolen: my wallet's been stolen me han robado la cartera [meh an ...]
stop: stop! ¡deténgase! [deh-t*e*nga-seh]
street una calle [k*a*-yeh]
strong fuerte [fw*ai*rteh]
student estudiante [esstood-y*a*nteh]
sugar azúcar [ath*oo*–]
suitcase una maleta [–l*e*h–]
sun el sol
sunburn una quemadura solar [keh-mad*oo*ra ...]
Sunday domingo
sunglasses unas gafas de sol
sunshade una sombrilla [som-br*ee*-ya]
sunstroke una insolación [–ath-yon]
suntan oil un bronceador [bronth*e*h-ador]
swim: I'm going for a swim me voy a dar un baño [... b*a*n-yoh]

....

table: a table for 4 una mesa para cuatro
  personas [... meh-sa para kwatroh pair– ...]
taxi un taxi
tea té [teh]
telegram un telegrama
telephone el teléfono [telleffonoh]
  number for UK is 07, wait for high-pitched tone,
  then 44 and drop first 0
tent una tienda de campaña [tee-enda deh
  kampan-ya]
terrible terrible [terreebleh]
thanks, thank you gracias [grath-yass]
  YOU MAY THEN HEAR ...
  de nada *you're welcome*
  no thank you no gracias
that ese; esa [eh-seh/eh-sa]
  that one ese [eh-seh]
  what's that? ¿qué es eso? [keh ess eh-soh]
the *(singular)* el; la *(plural)* los; las
them: with/for them con/para ellos [... eh-yoss]
there allí [a-yee]
  is there .../are there ...? ¿hay ...? [eye]
these estos; estas
they ellos; ellas [eh-yoss/eh-yass]
  are they ...? ¿son ...?
thirsty: I'm thirsty tengo sed [... seth]
this este; esta; **is this ...?** ¿es esto ...?
those esos; esas
Thursday jueves [hweh-vess]
ticket un billete [beeyeh-teh]
time el tiempo [tee-empoh]; *see pages 124–125*
tired cansado
tissues kleenex
to: to Madrid a Madrid [ah madree ...]
today hoy [oy]
together junto [hoontoh]
toilet los aseos [ass-eh-oss]
tomorrow mañana [man-yah-na]
  the day after tomorrow pasado mañana
tonight esta noche [... notcheh]

too demasiado [demass-yah-doh]
  me too yo también [tamb-yen]
tour un viaje [vee-ah-heh]
tourist un turista [tooreess-ta]
tourist office la oficina de turismo [offeetheena deh tooreezmoh]
towel una toalla [toh-ah-ya]
town una ciudad [thee-ooda]
  (*smaller*) un pueblo [pweh-bloh]
train el tren
translate traducir [–ootheer]
travel agent's una agencia de viajes [ahenth-ya deh vee-ah-hess]
trousers unos pantalones [–loh-ness]
try probar
Tuesday martes [–tess]
twice dos veces [... vethess]
understand: I don't understand no entiendo [noh ent-yendoh]
urgent urgente [oor-henteh]
us: for us para nosotros [... nossoh-tross]
use: can I use ...? ¿puedo usar ...? [pweh-doh oosar]
vegetarian vegetariano [vehetarree-ah-noh]
very muy [mwee]
  very much mucho [moo–]
village un pueblo [pweh-bloh]
wait: I'm waiting for a friend estoy esperando a un amigo
wake: will you wake me up at 7.30? ¿quiere despertarme a las siete y media? [kee-eh-reh dess-pair-tarmeh ah lass see-eh-teh ee maid-ya]
Wales Gales [gah-less]
want: I want a ... quiero un/una ... [kee-eh-roh ...]
  I don't want to no quiero (hacerlo) [noh kee-eh-roh ath-air-loh]
warm: it's warm today hoy hace calor [oy ah-theh ...]
water agua [ahg-wa]
we nosotros [nossoh-tross]; **we are ...** somos ...

....

Wednesday miércoles [mee-*air*-koless]
week una semana
well: how are you? – very well, thanks ¿cómo
  está usted? – muy bien, gracias [... oos*teh* mwee
  bee-*e*n grath-yass]
wet mojado [mo*hah*-doh]
what? ¿qué? [keh]
when? ¿cuándo? [kw*a*ndoh]
where? ¿dónde? [dondeh]
  where is ...? ¿dónde está ...?
which: which one? ¿cuál? [kwal]
white blanco
who? ¿quién? [kee-*e*n]
why? ¿por qué? [... keh]
  why not? ¿por qué no?
wife: my wife mi mujer [mee moo-*hair*]
window la ventana
windsurfing el windsurf
wine vino
with con
without sin [seen]
woman una mujer [moo-*hair*]
work: it's not working no funciona
  [foonth-y*o*nah]
write escribir [esskreeb*ee*r]
  could you write it down? ¿puede
  escribírmelo? [pw*e*h-deh esskreeb*ee*r-meh-loh]
wrong: there's something wrong here aquí
  hay algún error [ak*ee* eye alg*oo*n eh-ror]
  what's wrong? ¿qué pasa? [keh ...]
year un año [*a*n-yoh]
yes sí [see]
yesterday ayer [ah-y*air*]
you usted [oos*teh*]
  (*for people you know well*) tú
  are you ...? ¿es usted .../eres ...? [... eh-ress]
young joven [*h*oh-ven]
your su/tu [soo/too]
youth hostel albergue juvenil [al-b*air*-gheh
  *h*oov*eh*-nee*l*]

0 cero [theh-roh]

1 uno [oonoh]	6 seis [sayss]
2 dos [doss]	7 siete [see-eh-teh]
3 tres [tress]	8 ocho [otchoh]
4 cuatro [kw–]	9 nueve [nweh-veh]
5 cinco [theen-koh]	10 diez [dee-eth]

11 once [on-theh]
12 doce [doh-theh]
13 trece [treh-theh]
14 catorce [kator-theh]
15 quince [keen-theh]
16 dieciseis [dee-ethee-sayss]
17 diecisiete [dee-ethee-see-eh-teh]
18 dieciocho [dee-ethee-otchoh]
19 diecinueve [dee-ethee-nweh-veh]
20 veinte [vain-teh]
21 veintiuno
30 treinta [train-ta]
31 treinta y uno [traint-eye-oonoh]
40 cuarenta [kw–]
50 cincuenta [theen-kwenta]

60 sesenta	70 setenta
80 ochenta	90 noventa
100 cien [thee-en]	101 ciento uno [thee-entoh...]

165 ciento sesenta y cinco
200 doscientos [doss-thee-entoss]
300 trescientos [tress-thee-entoss]
400 cuatrocientos [kwatroh-thee-entoss]
500 quinientos [keen-yentoss]
600 seiscientos [sayss-thee-entoss]
700 setecientos [seh-teh-thee-entoss]
800 ochocientos [otchoh-thee-entoss]
900 novecientos [noveh-thee-entoss]
1,000 mil [meel]   2,000 dos mil
4,653 cuatro mil seiscientos cincuenta y tres
1,000,000 un millón [meel-yon]

for thousands use a full-stop: 3.000
for decimals use a comma: 4,6 [... koma ...]

Starters
cocktail de gambas *prawn cocktail*
zumo de tomate *tomato juice*
espárragos con mayonesa *asparagus with mayonnaise*
ensaladilla rusa *Russian salad*
ensalada mixta *mixed salad*
entremeses variados *mixed hors d'oeuvres*
croquetas *croquettes*

Sopas: Soups
gazpacho *refreshingly cold purée of tomato, bread, oil and vinegar with garlic and peppers*
consomé *clear soup*
sopa Juliana *shredded vegetable soup*
sopa sevillana *fish and mayonnaise*
crema de champiñones *cream of mushroom*
sopa de cebolla *onion with bread, cheese*

Verduras: Vegetable dishes
alcachofas salteadas con jamón *sautéed artichokes with ham*
fabada asturiana *butter beans with salami-type sausage*
menestra *stew of broad beans and other vegetables*
habas con jamón *broad beans fried with ham*

Carnes: Meat dishes
entrecot a la parrilla *grilled steak*
escalope Milanesa *escalope of veal fried in white sauce and bread crumbs*
albóndigas *meatballs in sauce*
pierna de cordero *leg of lamb*
chuletas de cerdo *pork chops*
filete de ternera *beef steak*
lomo al ajillo *pork loin in garlic*
riñones al Jerez *kidneys in sherry sauce*

Aves y caza: Fowl and game
pollo asado *roast chicken*

gallina en pepitoria *chicken casserole with almonds, garlic etc*
pato a la naranja *duck in orange sauce*
perdiz/faisán/codorniz *partridge, pheasant, quail*

Pescado: Fish
merluza *hake*
mero *sea-bream*
lenguado *sole*
boquerones fritos *fresh anchovies fried*
calamares fritos *squid fried in batter*
calamares en su tinta *squid in its ink*
gambas a la plancha *grilled scampi*
pez espada *sword-fish*
trucha *trout*

Huevos: Egg dishes
tortilla española *potato omelette*
tortilla francesa *plain omelette*
tortilla de jamón *ham omelette*
huevos a la flamenca *eggs baked in tomato, ham, onion, asparagus, sausage*
huevos al plato *eggs baked in oven*
huevos fritos con jamón *fried eggs and gammon*
arroz a la cubana *fried eggs and banana with rice and tomato purée*

Others
paella *rice, shellfish, meat, peas, tomato, red peppers and saffron*
cocido *chick-pea stew, sausage and vegetables*

Postres: Desserts
fruta del tiempo *seasonal fruit*
piña *pineapple*
melocotón en almíbar *peach in syrup*
flan *caramel custard*
tarta helada *multi-layered ice cream*
pijama *caramel custard, ice cream, fruit and syrup*

ITALIAN

Letters printed in italics show which part of a word should be stressed.

buon viaggio!
[bwon vee-*ah*-joh]
have a good trip!

a, an un, una [oon, *oo*-nah]
accident un incidente [een-chee-den-tay]
adaptor una spina multipla [spee-nah
  mool-tee-plah]
address l'indirizzo [een-dee-reet-tzoh]
after dopo
afternoon il pomeriggio [po-may-ree-joh]
  good afternoon (*from morning till
  mid-afternoon*) buon giorno [bwon jor-noh]
  (*after that*) buona sera [bwo-nah *say*-rah]
again ancora
airport l'aeroporto [ah-ay-ro-por-toh]
all tutto [*toot*-toh]
  all night tutta la notte [–tay]
  all right va bene [... b*ay*-nay]
almost quasi [kw*ah*-see]
alone solo
always sempre [s*em*-pray]
and e [ay]
another un altro
arrive arrivare [ar-ree-v*ah*-ray]
ashtray un portacenere [por-ta-ch*ay*-nay-ray]
ask chiedere [kee-*ay*-day-ray]
  could you ask him to ...? può chiedergli di ...?
  [pwoh kee-*ay*-der-lee dee ...]
baby il bambino
back: I'll be back soon torno subito
  [... s*oo*-bee-toh]
bad cattivo [kat-*tee*-voh]
  it's not bad non c'è male [non cheh m*ah*-lay]
bag una borsa; (*handbag*) una borsetta
bank la banca
bar il bar
bath un bagno [b*an*-yoh]
bathroom il bagno [b*an*-yoh]
beach la spiaggia [spee-*ah*-jah]
beautiful bello
because perché [per-k*ay*]
bed il letto
beer una birra [b*eer*-rah]

before prima (di) [pree-mah (dee)]
best migliore [meel-yoh-ray]
better meglio [mel-yoh]
bicycle la bicicletta [bee-chee-klayt-tah]
big grande [–day]
bill il conto
black nero [nay-roh]
blanket una coperta
blue blu
boat una barca
book un libro [lee-broh]
boring noioso [no-yoh-soh]
both entrambi [en-tram-bee]
bottle una bottiglia [bot-teel-yah]
boy il ragazzo [ra-gat-tzoh]
brake il freno [fray-noh]
bread il pane [pah-nay]
breakfast la colazione [ko-la-tzee-oh-nay]
broken rotto
brother: my brother mio fratello [mee-oh ...]
bus l'autobus [ow-toh-boos]
bus stop la fermata dell'autobus
butter il burro [boor-roh]
café un caffè [kaf-feh]
camera la macchina fotografica [mak-kee-nah]
campsite un camping
can: can I have ...? posso avere ...? [... a-vay-ray]
  can you ...? può ...? [pwoh]
  I can't ... non posso ...
cancel cancellare [kan-chel-lah-ray]
car l'auto [ow-toh], la macchina [mak-kee-nah]
car park un parcheggio [par-kay-joh]
centre il centro [chen-troh]
change: can you change this into lire? può
  cambiare questi in lire? [pwoh
  kam-bee-ah-ray ...]
  I want to change my reservation desidero
  cambiare la prenotazione [day-see-day-roh ...]
cheap a buon mercato [ah bwon mayr-kah-toh]
cheers salute [–tay]

....

cheese il formaggio [for-*mah*-joh]
chemist's la farmacia [far-ma-*chee*-ah]
cheque un assegno [as-*sayn*-yoh]
children i bambini [ee bam-*bee*-nee]
chips le patatine fritte [pa-ta-*tee*-nay freet-tay]
church la chiesa [kee-*ay*-sah]
cigar un sigaro [*see*-ga-roh]
cigarette una sigaretta
clean pulito [poo-*lee*-toh]
clothes i vestiti [ee ves-*tee*-tee]
coat il cappotto
coffee un caffè [kaf-*feh*]
  white coffee un cappuccino
  [kap-poo-ch*ee*-noh]
cold freddo
comb un pettine [pet-*tee*-nay]
come venire [vay-*nee*-ray]
  come on! andiamo!
  come here vieni qui [vee-*ay*-nee kwee]
constipation la stitichezza [stee-tee-k*ayt*-tzah]
consul il console [kon-so-lay]
cost: what does it cost? quanto costa?
could: could you please ...? potrebbe ...?
  [po-tr*ayb*-bay]
  could I have ...? potrei avere ...? [po-tr*ay*
  a-v*ay*-ray]
crazy: you're crazy lei è pazzo
  [lay eh p*at*-tzoh]
crisps le patatine [pa-ta-*tee*-nay]
Customs la Dogana
dark scuro
daughter: my daughter mia figlia [*feel*-yah]
delicious delizioso [day-lee-tzee-*oh*-soh]
dentist il dentista
develop: could you develop these? può
  sviluppare questi? [pwoh svee-loop-p*ah*-ray ...]
different: a different room un'altra camera
  [... k*ah*-may-rah]
difficult difficile [deef-*fee*-chee-lay]
dinner la cena [ch*ay*-nah]

do fare [fah-ray]
  how do you do? piacere [pee-a-chay-ray]
doctor il medico [meh-dee-koh]
door la porta
dress un vestito [ves-tee-toh]
drink: something to drink qualcosa da bere
  [... bay-ray]
driving licence la patente [pa-ten-tay]
drunk ubriaco [oo-bree-ah-koh]
dry-cleaner's un lavasecco
early presto
easy facile [fah-chee-lay]
eat: something to eat qualcosa da mangiare
  [... man-jah-ray]
else: something else qualcos'altro
England l'Inghilterra [een-gheel-ter-rah]
English inglese [een-glay-say]
enough basta
entertainment il divertimento [dee-vayr-tee–]
evening la sera [say-rah]
  this evening stasera
  good evening buona sera [bwo-nah ...]
everyone tutti [toot-tee]
everything tutto [toot-toh]
excellent eccellente [ay-chayl-len-tay]
excuse me (to get past) permesso
  (to get attention) scusi [skoo-zee]
expensive costoso
far: how far is it? quanto dista? [... dees-tah]
fast veloce [vay-loh-chay]
  don't speak so fast non parli così in fretta
  [... ko-see ...]
father: my father mio padre [mee-oh pah-dray]
ferry il traghetto [tra-gayt-toh]
few: only a few solo pochi [... po-kee]
film (movie) un film [feelm]
  do you have this type of film? avete questo
  tipo di pellicola? [a-vay-tay kwes-toh tee-poh
  dee payl-lee-ko-lah]
first primo [pree-moh]

....

food il cibo [ch*ee*-boh]
for per [payr]
fork la forchetta [for-k*ay*t-tah]
free libero [l*ee*-bay-roh]; (*no charge*) gratis
Friday venerdì [vay-nayr-d*ee*]
friend un amico [a-m*ee*-koh]
from da
fun: it's fun è divertente [eh dee-vayr-t*en*-tay]
funny (*comical*) buffo [b*oof*-foh]
　　(*strange*) strano [str*ah*-noh]
garage il garage [ga-r*ah*-jay]
girl una ragazza [ra-g*at*-tzah]
give dare [d*ah*-ray]
glasses gli occhiali [ok-y*ah*-lee]
go andare [an-d*ah*-ray]
　　he's gone è andato via [eh ... v*ee*-ah]
good buono [bw*o*-noh]
　　good! bene! [b*ay*-nay]
goodbye arrivederci [ar-ree-vay-d*ay*r-chee]
guide una guida [gw*ee*-dah]
hairdresser's un parrucchiere
　　[par-rook-y*ay*-ray]
handbag la borsetta [bor-s*ay*t-tah]
happy contento
harbour il porto
hard duro [d*oo*-roh]
have avere [a-v*ay*-ray]
　　do you have ...? ha ...? [ah]
　　I don't have ... non ho ... [... o]
he lui [l*oo*-ee]; **is he ...?** è ...? [eh]
headache il mal di testa [... dee ...]
hello ciao [chow]
help: can you help me? mi può aiutare? [mee
　　pwoh a-yoo-t*ah*-ray]
her: for her per lei [... lay]
　　it's her bag/plate è la sua borsa/il suo piatto
here qui [kwee]
him: for him per lui [... l*oo*-ee]
his il suo [s*oo*-oh]; la sua
holiday una vacanza [va-kan-tzah]

home la casa [k*ah*-sah]
  at home a casa
hospital l'ospedale [os-pay-d*ah*-lay]
hot caldo; (*spiced*) piccante [peek-k*an*-tay]
hotel l'albergo
hour l'ora
house la casa [k*ah*-sah]
how? come? [k*oh*-may]
  how many? quanti? [kwan-tee]
  how much? quanto? [kwan-toh]
  how are you? come sta? [k*oh*-may stah]
hungry: I'm hungry/not hungry ho fame/non ho fame [o f*ah*-may ...]
hurt: it hurts fa male [fah m*ah*-lay]
husband: my husband mio marito [m*ee*-oh ma-r*ee*-toh]
I io [*ee*-oh]; **I am ...** sono ...
ice il ghiaccio [ghee-*ah*-choh]
ice cream un gelato [jay-l*ah*-toh]
if se [say]
ill malato
immediately immediatamente [–tay]
important importante [–tay]
in in [een]
Ireland l'Irl*a*nda
it esso; **is it ...?** è ...? [eh]
Italian italiano
  the Italians gli italiani [lee ...]
Italy l'Italia [ee-t*a*l-yah]
jacket una giacca [j*a*k-kah]
just: just a little solo un po'
key la chiave [kee-*ah*-vay]
kiss un bacio [b*ah*-choh]
knife il coltello [kol-t*e*l-loh]
know: I don't know non so
last ultimo [*oo*l-tee-moh]
  last night la notte scorsa [–tay ...]
late tardi [t*a*r-dee]
later più tardi [pew ...]
  see you later a più tardi

....

leave: we leave tomorrow partiamo domani
  when does the bus leave? quando parte
  l'autobus? [... par-tay low-toh-boos]
  I left two shirts in my room ho lasciato due
  camicie in camera mia [o la-shah-toh doo-ay
  ka-mee-chay een kah-may-rah mee-ah]
  can I leave this here? posso lasciarlo qua?
  [... la-shahr-loh ...]
left: on the left a sinistra [see-nees-trah]
left luggage (office) il deposito bagagli
  [day-po-see-toh ba-gal-yee]
letter la lettera [let-tay-rah]
light la luce [loo-chay]
have you got a light? ha da accendere? [ah da
  a-chen-day-ray]
like: would you like ...? vuole ...? [vwoh-lay]
  I'd like a ... vorrei un ... [vor-ray oon]
  I'd like to go vorrei partire [... –tee-ray]
  I like it/I don't like it mi piace/non mi piace
  [... mee pee-ah-chay]
little piccolo
  a little un po'
lorry l'autocarro [ow-toh-kar-roh]
lose: I've lost my ... ho perso il mio ... [o payr-soh
  eel mee-oh]
  I'm lost mi sono perso [mee ...]
lot: a lot/not a lot molto/non molto
luggage il bagaglio [ba-gal-yoh]
lunch il pranzo [pran-tzoh]
main road la strada principale
  [... preen-chee-pah-lay]
man un uomo [wo-moh]
manager il direttore [dee-ray-toh-ray]
map: a map of Italy una carta d'Italia
  a map of Rome una pianta di Roma
  [pee-an-tah dee ...]
market il mercato [mayr-kah-toh]
match: a box of matches una scatola di
  fiammiferi [skah-toh-lah dee
  fee-am-mee-fay-ree]

matter: it doesn't matter non importa
maybe forse [for-say]
me: with me con me [kon may]
mean: what does this mean? cosa vuol dire?
[... vwol dee-ray]
menu il menù [may-noo]
milk il latte [lat-tay]
mine mio [mee-oh]
mineral water l'acqua minerale [–rah-lay]
minute minuto [mee-noo-toh]
Monday lunedì [loo-nay-dee]
money il denaro [day-nah-roh]
more più [pew]
   more wine, please ancora del vino per favore
   [an-koh-ra del vee-noh payr fa-voh-ray]
morning il mattino [–tee-noh]
   good morning buon giorno [bwon jor-noh]
mother: my mother mia madre [mee-ah
   mah-dray]
motorbike la motocicletta [–chee-klayt-tah]
motorway l'autostrada [ow-toh-strah-dah]
mountain la montagna [mon-tan-yah]
much molto
   not much non molto
music la musica [moo-see-kah]
must: I must ... devo ... [day-voh]
   I must not ... non devo ...
   you must do it deve farlo [day-vay ...]
my il mio [mee-oh]; la mia; (plural) i miei [ee
   mee-eh-ee]; le mie [–ay]
name il nome [noh-may]
   my name is ... mi chiamo ... [mee kee-ah-moh]
   what's your name? come si chiama? [koh-may
   see kee-ah-mah]
near: is it near? è vicino? [eh vee-chee-noh]
necessary necessario [nay-chays-sah-ree-oh]
needle un ago [ah-goh]
never mai [my]
new nuovo [nwo-voh]
newspaper il giornale [jor-nah-lay]

next prossimo [pros-see-moh]
nice bello
  (*person*) simpatico [... seem-p*ah*-tee-koh]
night la notte [n*o*t-tay]
  good night buona notte [bw*o*-nah ...]
no no
  there's no water non c'è acqua [non cheh ...]
nobody nessuno
noisy rumoroso
not non
  not me io no [*ee*-oh ...]
  not that one non quello
nothing niente [nee-*en*-tay]
now adesso
nowhere da nessuna parte [... p*ar*-tay]
number il numero [n*oo*-may-roh]
of di [dee]
often spesso
oil l'olio [*o*l-yoh]
OK okay
old vecchio [v*ek*-yoh]
on su [soo]
one uno
only solo
open aperto
or o
orange juice succo d'arancia [s*oo*k-koh
  da-r*an*-chah]
other: the other one quell'altro
our il nostro; la nostra
over: over here/there qui/la [kwee/lah]
pain il dolore [doh-l*oh*-ray]
painkillers gli antidolorifici [lee
  an-tee-doh-loh-r*ee*-fee-chee]
paper la carta
pardon? come? [k*oh*-may]
passport il passaporto
pen una penna
people la gente [j*en*-tay]
petrol la benzina [ben-tz*ee*-nah]

. . . .

photograph la fotografia [–*fee*-ah]
piece il pezzo [pet-tzoh]
plane l'aereo [ah-*eh*-ray-oh]
platform: which platform? che binario? [kay bee-n*ah*-ree-oh]
please per favore [payr fa-v*oh*-ray]
  yes, please sì, grazie [see gr*ah*-tzee-ay]
police la polizia [po-lee-tz*ee*-ah]
pool (*swimming*) la piscina [pee-sh*ee*-nah]
pope il papa
possible possibile [pos-*see*-bee-lay]
postcard la cartolina [kar-toh-l*ee*-nah]
post office l'ufficio postale [oof-*fee*-choh pos-t*ah*-lay]
pretty carino [ka-r*ee*-noh]
problem il problema [pro-bl*ay*-mah]
pronounce: how do you pronounce this? come si pronuncia? [k*oh*-may see pro-n*oo*n-chah]
purse il borsellino [–*ee*-noh]
quiet quieto [kwee-*ay*-toh]
quite (*fairly*) assai [as-s*ah*-ee]
rain: it's raining piove [pee-*o*-vay]
ready: when will it be ready? per quando è pronto? [... eh ...]
receipt una ricevuta [ree-chay-v*oo*-tah]
red rosso
rent: can I rent a car? posso affittare una macchina? [... af-feet-t*ah*-ray *oo*-nah m*a*k-kee-nah]
repair: can you repair it? può ripararlo? [pwoh ...]
reservation la prenotazione [pray-no-ta-tzee-*oh*-nay]
restaurant il ristorante [–*tay*]
return: a return to ... un'andata e [ay] rit*o*rno per ...
right: on the right a destra
  that's right sì, esatto
river il fiume [f*ew*-may]
road la strada

....

room la camera [k*ah*-may-rah]
   have you got a (single/double) room? ha una
   camera (singola/doppia)? [ah ...
   s*ee*n-go-lah/dop-pee-ah]
   for one night/three nights per una notte/per
   tre notti [... n*o*t-tay/... n*o*t-tee]
safe sicuro [see-k*oo*-roh]
salt il sale [s*ah*-lay]
same stesso
   the same again ancora dello stesso
Saturday sabato [s*ah*-ba-toh]
say: how do you say ... in Italian? come si dice
   in italiano ...? [k*oh*-may see d*ee*-chay ...]
   what did he say? cosa ha detto? [... ah ...]
scissors forbici [for-bee-chee]
Scotland la Scozia [sk*o*-tzee-ah]
sea il mare [m*ah*-ray]
seat un posto a sedere [... say-d*a*y-ray]
see vedere [vay-d*a*y-ray]
   can I see the room? posso vedere la camera?
   I see (*understand*) ho capito [o ka-p*ee*-toh]
send spedire [spay-d*ee*-ray]
shampoo lo shampoo [sh*a*m-poh]
she lei [lay]; **is she ...?** è ...? [eh]
shirt la camicia [ka-m*ee*-chah]
shoes le scarpe [sk*a*r-pay]
shop il negozio [nay-go-tzee-oh]
show: please show me mi può mostrare? [mee
   pwoh mos-tr*ah*-ray]
shower: with shower con doccia [d*o*h-chah]
shut chiuso [kee-*oo*-soh]
single: a single to ... un'andata per ... [oon
   an-d*ah*-tah ...]
sister: my sister mia sorella [m*ee*-ah ...]
sit: can I sit here? posso sedermi qui?
   [... say-d*a*yr-mee kwee]
skirt la gonna
slow: could you speak a little slower? può
   parlare un po' più lentamente? [pwoh
   par-l*ah*-ray oon po pew len-ta-m*a*yn-tay]

small piccolo
so così [ko-s*ee*]
   not so much non così tanto
soap il sapone [sa-p*oh*-nay]
somebody qualcuno [kwal-k*oo*-noh]
something qualcosa
son: my son mio figlio [*mee*-oh f*ee*l-yoh]
soon presto
sorry: (I'm) sorry mi spiace [mee spee-*ah*-chay]
souvenir un souvenir
speak: do you speak English? parla l'inglese?
   [... leen-gl*ay*-say]
   I don't speak Italian non parlo l'italiano
spoon il cucchiaio [kook-y*ah*-yoh]
stairs le scale [lay sk*ah*-lay]
stamp il francobollo [fran-ko-b*ol*-loh]
   two stamps for England due francobolli per
   l'Inghilterra [*doo*-ay ... payr leen-gheel-*ter*-rah]
station la stazione [sta-tzee-*oh*-nay]
sticking plaster il cerotto [chay-r*ot*-toh]
stolen: my wallet's been stolen mi hanno
   rubato il portafoglio [mee *a*n-noh roo-b*ah*-toh
   eel por-ta-f*ol*-yoh]
stop! ferma!
street la strada
strong forte [f*or*-tay]
student uno studente [stoo-d*en*-tay]
sugar lo zucchero [tz*oo*-kay-roh]
suitcase una valigia [va-l*ee*-jah]
sun il sole [s*oh*-lay]
sunburn la scottatura [skot-ta-t*oo*-rah]
Sunday domenica [doh-m*ay*-nee-kah]
sunglasses gli occhiali da sole [lee ok-y*ah*-lee
   dah s*oh*-lay]
sunshade un ombrellone [om-brel-l*oh*-nay]
sunstroke il colpo di [dee] sole
suntan oil l'olio solare [l*ol*-yoh so-l*ah*-ray]
swim: I'm going for a swim vado a fare una
   nuotata [v*ah*-doh ah f*ah*-ray *oo*-nah
   nwo-t*ah*-tah]

table: a table for 4 un tavolo per quattro [oon *tah*-vo-loh payr ...]
taxi il tassì [tas-*see*]
tea il tè [teh]
telegram il telegramma
telephone il telefono [tay-l*eh*-fo-noh]
number for UK is 0044 and drop first 0 of area code
tent la tenda
terrible terribile [ter-*ree*-bee-lay]
thank you grazie [*grah*-tzee-ay]
YOU MAY THEN HEAR ...
prego *you're welcome*
no thank you no grazie
that quello; quella
  that one quello
the (*singular*) il, lo; la
  (*plural*) i [ee], gli [lee]; le [lay]
them: with them con loro
there lì [lee]
  is there/are there ...? c'è .../ci sono ...? [cheh/chee *soh*-noh]
these questi; queste
they essi [*es*-see]; **are they ...?** sono ...?
thirsty: I'm thirsty ho sete [o *say*-tay]
this questo; questa
  can I have this one? posso avere questo?
  is this ...? è questo ...? [eh ...]
those quelli; quelle [kw*ay*l-lee kw*ay*l-lay]
Thursday giovedì [jo-vay-*dee*]
ticket il biglietto [beel-*yet*-toh]
  (*cloakroom*) lo scontrino [skon-*tree*-noh]
time il tempo; *see pages 124–125*
tired stanco
tissues i fazzolettini di carta [ee fat-tzoh-let-*tee*-nee dee ...]
to: to Rome/England a Roma/in Inghilterra
today oggi [*o*-jee]
together insieme [een-see-*ay*-may]
toilet la toilette [twa-let]

tomorrow domani [doh-m*ah*-nee]
  the day after tomorrow dopodomani
tonight stasera [stah-s*ay*-rah]
too troppo; (*also*) anche [*an*-kay]
tour un viaggio [vee-*ah*-joh]
tourist un turista
tourist office l'ufficio turistico [oof-*fee*-choh
  too-r*ees*-tee-koh]
towel un asciugamano [a-shoo-ga-m*ah*-noh]
town la città [cheet-t*ah*]
train il treno
translate tradurre [tra-d*oor*-ray]
travel agency l'agenzia di viaggi [a-jen-tz*ee*-ah
  dee vee-*ah*-jee]
trousers i pantaloni
try provare [pro-v*ah*-ray]
  can I try it? posso provarlo?
Tuesday martedì [mar-tay-d*ee*]
twice due volte [d*oo*-ay vol-tay]
umbrella l'ombrello
understand: I don't understand non capisco
  [... ka-p*ees*-koh]
urgent urgente [oor-jen-tay]
us: for us per noi [payr noy]
use: can I use ...? posso adoperare ...? [–r*ah*-ray]
vegetarian un vegetariano
  [vay-jay-ta-ree-*ah*-noh]
very molto
  very much moltissimo
village il villaggio [veel-l*ah*-joh]
wait: I'm waiting for a friend aspetto un amico
  [... oon a-m*ee*-koh]
wake: will you wake me at 7.30? mi sveglia alle
  sette e mezza? [mee sv*el*-yah *al*-lay s*et*-tay ay
  met-tzah]
Wales il Galles [g*al*-lays]
want: I want a ... voglio un ... [v*ol*-yoh oon]
  I don't want to non ne ho voglia [non nay o
  v*ol*-yah]
warm caldo

....

water l'acqua
we noi [noy]; **we are ...** siamo ... [see-*ah*-moh]
Wednesday mercoledì [mer-ko-lay-*dee*]
week la settimana
well: how are you? – very well, thanks come
  sta? – bene, grazie [k*oh*-may stah – b*ay*-nay
  gr*ah*-tzee-ay]
wet bagnato [ban-y*ah*-toh]
what? cosa?
when? quando?
where? dove? [d*oh*-vay]
  where is ...? dov'è ...? [doh-v*eh*]
which? quale? [kw*ah*-lay]
white bianco [bee-*a*n-koh]
who? chi? [kee]
why? perché? [payr-k*ay*]
  why not? perché no?
wife: my wife mia moglie [m*ee*-ah m*o*l-yay]
window la finestra [fee-n*e*s-trah]
wine il vino [v*ee*-noh]
with con
without senza [s*e*n-tzah]
woman la donna
work: it's not working non funziona
  [... foon-tzee-*oh*-nah]
write scrivere [skr*ee*-vay-ray]
  could you write it down? può scriverlo?
  [pwoh ...]
wrong sbagliato [sbal-y*ah*-toh]
  what's wrong? cosa succede? [... soo-ch*ay*-day]
year l'anno
yes sì [see]
yesterday ieri [y*eh*-ree]
you lei [lay]
  (*to somebody you know well*) tu [too]
  are you ...? è .../sei ...? [eh/say]
young giovane [j*oh*-va-nay]
your suo [s*oo*-oh]; tuo [t*oo*-oh]
youth hostel l'ostello della gioventù
  [... jo-ven-t*oo*]

 0 zero [tzay-roh]

1 uno [oo-noh]	6 sei [say]
2 due [doo-ay]	7 sette [set-tay]
3 tre [tray]	8 otto
4 quattro	9 nove [no-vay]
5 cinque [cheen-kway]	10 dieci [dee-eh-chee]

11 undici [oon-dee-chee]
12 dodici [doh-dee-chee]
13 tredici [tray-dee-chee]
14 quattordici [kwat-tor-dee-chee]
15 quindici [kween-dee-chee]
16 sedici [say-dee-chee]
17 diciassette [dee-chas-set-tay]
18 diciotto [dee-chot-toh]
19 diciannove [dee-chan-no-vay]

20 venti	29 ventinove
21 ventuno	30 trenta
22 ventidue	31 trentuno
23 ventitré	40 quaranta
24 ventiquattro	50 cinquanta
25 venticinque	60 sessanta
26 ventisei	70 settanta
27 ventisette	80 ottanta
28 ventotto	90 novanta

100 cento [chen-toh]
101 centouno [chen-toh-oo-noh]
165 centosessantacinque
200 duecento
300 trecento
400 quattrocento
500 cinquecento
1,000 mille [meel-lay]
2,000 duemila [doo-ay-mee-lah]
4,653 quattromilaseicentocinquantatre
1,000,000 un milione
1,000,000,000 un miliardo

for thousands use a full-stop: 4.000
for decimals use a comma: 4,6 [... ay ...]

Antipasti: Starters
affettati misti *assorted cold meats*
prosciutto e melone *ham and melon*
insalata di frutti di mare *seafood salad*

Primi piatti: Soups and pasta
stracciatella *clear soup with eggs and cheese*
minestrone *thick vegetable soup*
zuppa di pesce *fish soup*
spaghetti alla carbonara *with egg and bacon
   sauce*
spaghetti al sugo *with meat sauce*
spaghetti al pomodoro *with tomato sauce*
lasagne al forno *layers of pasta and meat sauce
   covered with cheese and baked*
cannelloni *pasta stuffed with meat sauce and
   baked*
ravioli *pasta squares stuffed with meat or other
   savoury filling, served with a sauce*
gnocchi *potato dumplings*
risotto alla milanese *rice cooked in white wine and
   saffron with mushrooms and cheese*

Carni: Meat dishes
bistecca ai ferri/alla pizzaiola/alla fiorentina
   *grilled steak/steak with tomato sauce/grilled
   T-bone steak*
cotoletta alla milanese *veal cutlet in egg and
   breadcrumbs*
cotoletta d'agnello/di vitello *lamb/veal cutlet*
ossobuco *knuckle of veal in wine and tomato sauce*
saltimbocca alla romana *veal escalopes with ham
   and sage*
spezzatino di vitello *veal stew*

Pollame: Poultry
anitra all'arancio *duck in orange sauce*
pollo arrosto *roast chicken*
pollo alla cacciatora *chicken in a wine, onion and
   tomato sauce*

Pesce: Fish
baccalà *salt cod*
calamari in umido *squid in wine, garlic and
   tomato sauce*
fritto misto *mixed fried fish*
pesce spada *sword-fish*
polipo ai ferri *grilled octopus*
sogliola al burro *sole in butter sauce*
trota ai ferri *grilled trout*

Contorni: Vegetables
patate: arrosto/fritte/cotte *potatoes:
   roast/fried/boiled*
puré di patate *mashed potatoes*
insalata mista *mixed salad*
pomodori al gratin *grilled tomatoes*
fagiolini al burro *French beans in butter*
finocchi al forno *fennel with cheese, browned in
   the oven*
melanzane al forno *baked aubergines in cheese
   sauce*
zucchini fritti *fried courgettes*

Formaggi: Cheese
Bel Paese *soft, full fat cheese*
caciotta *hard, medium fat cheese*
gorgonzola *soft, tangy blue cheese*
mozzarella *soft, sweet cheese made from buffalo's
   milk*
parmigiano *Parmesan*

Frutta e dolci: Desserts
macedonia *fruit salad*
bignè *profiteroles*
cassata *ice cream with candied fruit*
gelato *ice cream*
torta di mele/ciliege etc *apple/cherry etc tart*
zabaione *frothy dessert made with egg yolks,
   sugar and marsala wine*
zuppa inglese *trifle*

PORTUGUESE

Special sounds in the pronunciation guide:

j   is like the second sound in 'measure' or 'seizure'

uh   is pronounced as in 'a' or the u in 'butter'

Letters printed in italics show which part of a word should be stressed. Feminine forms, where noticeably different from the masculine, are given after an oblique.

boa viagem!
[bo-uh vee-*ah*-jeng]
have a good trip!

....

a, an um, uma [oom, *oo*muh]
accident um acidente [asseed*e*nt]
adaptor um adaptador [adaptuh-d*o*r]
address o endereço [endereh-soo]
after depois [dep*oi*sh]
afternoon a tarde [tard]
   good afternoon boa tarde [b*o*-uh tard]
again outra vez [*o*h-truh vesh]
airport o aeroporto [a-*ai*rooportoo]
all todo [toh-doo]
   all right muito bem [mw*ee*ntoo beng]
almost quase [kwahz]
alone só
always sempre [s*e*mpruh]
and e [ee]
another: another room um outro quarto [oom
   *o*h-troo kw*a*rtoo]
   another beer mais uma cerveja [myze *oo*muh
   serveh-juh]
arrive chegar [shuh-g*a*r]
ashtray o cinzeiro [seenz*a*yroo]
ask: could you ask him to ...? podia pedir-lhe
   para ...? [pood*ee*-uh ped*ee*r-lyuh para ...]
baby o bebé [bebeh]
back: I'll be back soon estou de volta em breve
   [shtoh duh v*o*ltuh aim brev]
bad mau/má [m*a*h-oo/mah]
bag um saco [s*a*ckoo]; (*case*) uma mala [m*a*h-luh]
bank o banco [oo b*a*nkoo]
bar um bar [bar]
bath um banho [b*a*n-yoo]
bathroom a casa de banho [k*a*h-zuh duh
   b*a*n-yoo]
beach a praia [pr*a*h-yuh]
beautiful lindo [l*ee*ndoo]
because porque [p*oo*r-kuh]
bed a cama [k*a*h-muh]
beer a cerveja [serveh-juh]
before antes de [*a*ntsh duh]
best o melhor [mul-y*o*r]

better melhor [mul-yor]
bicycle uma bicicleta [bee-see-kletta]
big grande [grand]
bill a conta [kontuh]
black preto [preh-too]
blanket um cobertor [koobertor]
blue azul [azool]
boat um barco [barkoo]
book um livro [leevroo]
boring maçador [massuh-dor]
both os dois [oosh doysh]
bottle uma garrafa [garrah-fuh]
boy um rapaz [rapash]
brake o travão [travowng]
bread pão [powng]
breakfast o pequeno almoço [pickeh-noo almo-soo]
broken partido [perteedoo]
brother irmão [eer-mowng]
bullfight uma tourada [toh-rah-duh]
bus um autocarro [owtoo-karro]
bus stop uma paragem de autocarro [oomuh parah-jeng dowtoo-karroo]
butter a manteiga [mantay-guh]
café um café [kuffeh]
camera uma máquina fotográfica [macky-nuh footoo-grafickuh]
campsite o parque de campismo [oo park duh kampeejmoo]
can: can I have ...? queria ... [kree-uh]
 can you ...? pode ...? [pod]
 I can't ... não posso ... [nowng possoo]
cancel cancelar [kanselar]
car o carro [karroo]
car park o estacionamento [shtass-yoonuh-mentoo]
centre o centro [sentroo]
change: could you change this into escudos? pode trocar isto por escudos? [pod trookar eeshtoo poor shkoodoosh]

....

I'd like to change my booking queria mudar a minha reserva [kr*ee*-uh mood*a*r uh m*ee*n-yuh rez*ai*rvuh]

cheap barato [bar*a*h-too]

cheers! saúde [suh-*oo*d]

cheese queijo [k*a*y-joo]

chemist's a farmácia [fur-m*a*ss-yuh]

cheque um cheque [sheck]

children filhos [f*ee*l-yoosh]

chips batatas fritas [bat*a*h-tush fr*ee*tush]

church a igreja [eegr*e*h-juh]

cigar um charuto [shar*oo*too]

cigarette um cigarro [see-g*a*rroo]

clean limpo [l*ee*m-poo]

clothes a roupa [r*o*h-puh]

coat um casaco [k*a*z*a*h-koo]

coffee café [k*u*ff*e*h]

    white coffee/black coffee um garoto/uma bica [oom gar*o*h-too/*o*omuh b*ee*kuh]

cold frio [fr*ee*-oo]

comb um pente [pent]

come vir [veer]

constipation prisão de ventre [preez*o*wng duh v*e*ntruh]

consul o cônsul [k*o*nsool]

cost: what does it cost? quanto custa? [kw*a*ntoo k*oo*shtuh]

could: could you please ...? pode ... por favor? [pod ... poor fuh-v*o*r]

    could I have ...? pode dar-me ...? [pod d*a*r-muh]

crazy doido [d*o*y-doo]

crisps batatas fritas [bat*a*h-tush fr*ee*-tush]

Customs Alfândega [al-f*a*n-dugguh]

dark escuro [shk*oo*roo]

daughter: my daughter minha filha [m*ee*n-yuh f*ee*l-yuh]

delicious delicioso [deleess-y*o*h-zoo]

dentist o dentista [dent*ee*shtuh]

develop: could you develop these? pode revelar-mas? [pod ruh-vel*a*r-mush]

different: a different room um outro quarto
  [oom *oh*-troo kw*ar*-too]
difficult difícil [dif*ee*-seel]
dinner o jantar [jant*ar*]
do: how do you do? muito prazer [mw*ee*ntoo
  praz*air*]
doctor o médico [m*e*ddikoo]
door a porta [p*or*-tuh]
dress um vestido [vesht*ee*doo]
drink: something to drink alguma coisa para
  beber [alg*oo*muh k*oy*-zuh para beb*air*]
driving licence a carta de condução [k*ar*tuh duh
  kondoo-s*ow*ng]
drunk bêbedo [b*e*bdoo]
dry-clean limpar a seco [leemp*ar* uh s*eh*-koo]
early cedo [s*eh*-doo]
easy fácil [f*ah*-seel]
eat: something to eat alguma coisa para comer
  [alg*oo*muh k*oy*-zuh para koo-m*air*]
else: something else uma outra coisa [*oo*muh
  oh-truh k*oy*-zuh]
England Inglaterra [eenglat*e*rruh]
English Inglês [eengl*e*sh]
enough: that's enough chega [sh*e*gguh]
entertainment divertimentos
  [deevertee-ment*oo*sh]
evening a tarde [t*ar*d]
  good evening boa tarde [b*o*-uh ...]
everyone toda a gente [t*oh*-dah jent]
everything tudo [t*oo*doo]
excellent excelente [eesh-s*e*lent]
excuse: excuse me (*to get past etc*) com licença
  [kong leesens*uh*]
  (*to get attention*) se faz favor [suh fash fuh-v*or*]
expensive caro [k*ah*-roo]
far: is it far? é longe? [eh lonj]
fast rápido [r*a*peedoo]
  don't speak so fast não fale tão depressa
  [n*ow*ng f*al* t*ow*ng duh-pr*e*ssuh]
father: my father meu pai [m*eh*-oo pye]

....

few: only a few só uns poucos [so oonsh poh-koosh]
film um filme [feelm]
   (*camera*) uma película [peleekooluh]
first primeiro [pree-may-roo]
fish peixe [paysh]
food a comida [koomeeduh]
for para
fork um garfo [garfoo]
free livre [leevruh]
   (*no cost*) gratuito [grat-weet-oo]
Friday sexta-feira [seshtuh fay-ruh]
friend um amigo [ameegoo]
from de [duh]
fun: it's fun é divertido [eh deeverteedoo]
funny (*strange*) estranho [shtran-yoo]
   (*comical*) engraçado [engrassah-doo]
garage (*repair*) uma garagem [garah-jeng]
   (*petrol*) uma estação de serviço [shtassowng duh servee-soo]
girl uma rapariga [ruppareeguh]
give dar
glasses óculos [ockooloosh]
go: I want to go to ... quero ir a ... [kairoo eer uh]
   he's gone foi-se embora [foy-suh embor-uh]
good bom/boa [bong/bo-uh]
   good! bom!
goodbye adeus [a-deh-oosh]
guide um guia [ghee-uh]
hairdresser's o cabeleireiro [kubbalay-ray-roo]
handbag uma mala de senhora [mah-luh duh sun-yoruh]
happy contente [kontent]
harbour o porto [portoo]
hard duro [dooroo]; (*difficult*) difícil [deefeeseel]
have ter [tair]
   do you have ...? tem ...? [teng]
   I have no ... não tenho ... [nowng ten-yoo]
he ele [ehl]; **is he ...?** é ...? [eh]
headache uma dor de cabeça [... duh kabeh-suh]

hello olá [o-lah]
help: can you help me? pode ajudar-me? [pod
ajoodar-muh]
her: with her com ela [kong elluh]
　it's her bag é o saco dela [eh oo sakoo delluh]
here aqui [akee]
him: with him com ele [kong ehl]
his: his drink a bebida dele [uh bebeeduh dehl]
holiday férias [fairy-ush]
home: at home em casa [eng kah-zuh]
hospital um hospital [o-shpeetal]
hot quente [kent]; (spiced) picante [peekant]
hotel um hotel [o-tel]
hour a hora [or-uh]
house a casa [kah-zuh]
how? como? [ko-moo]
　how many? quantos? [kwantoosh]
　how much? quanto?
　how are you? como está? [ko-moo shtah]
hungry: I'm hungry/not hungry tenho/não
tenho fome [ten-yoo/nowng ten-yoo fom]
hurt: it hurts dói-me [doy-muh]
husband: my husband o meu marido [oo meh-oo
mareedoo]
I eu [eh-oo]; **I am** sou ... [soh]
ice gelo [jeh-loo]
ice cream um gelado [jelah-doo]
if se [suh]
ill doente [doo-ent]
immediately imediatamente
　[eemuddy-ahtuh-ment]
important importante [eempoortant]
in em [eng]
Ireland Irlanda [eerlanduh]
it: is it ...? é ...? [eh]
jacket um casaco [kazah-koo]
just: just a little só um pouco [so oom poh-koo]
key a chave [shahv]
kiss um beijo [bay-joo]
knife uma faca [fah-kuh]

know: I don't know não sei [nowng say]
last último [ooltimoo]
  last night ontem à noite [onteng ah noyt]
late tarde [tard]
later mais tarde [mysh tard]
  see you later até logo [ateh loggoo]
leave: we're leaving tomorrow vamos partir
  amanhã [vamoosh per-teer a-man-yang]
  when does the bus leave? a que horas parte o
  autocarro? [uh kee orush part oo owtoo-karroo]
  I left two shirts in my room deixei duas
  camisas no meu quarto [day-shay doo-ush
  kameezush noo meh-oo kwartoo]
  can I leave this here? posso deixar isto aqui?
  [possoo day-shar eeshtoo akee]
left: on the left à esquerda [ah shkair-duh]
left luggage (office) o déposito de bagagem
  [depozitoo duh bagah-jeng]
letter uma carta [kartuh]
light a luz [loosh]
  have you got a light? tem lume, por favor?
  [teng loom poor fuh-vor]
like: would you like ...? gostaria de ...?
  [gooshtaree-uh duh]
  I'd like a .../I'd like to ... queria [kree-uh]
  I like it gosto disso [goshtoo dee-soo]
  I don't like it não gosto disso [nowng ...]
little pequeno [pickeh-noo]
  a little um bocadinho [oom bookadeen-yoo]
lorry um camião [kamee-owng]
lose: I've lost ... perdi ... [perdee]
  I'm lost estou perdido [shtoh perdeedoo]
lot: a lot/not a lot muito/não muito
  [mweentoo/nowng ...]
luggage a bagagem [bagah-jeng]
lunch o almoço [al-mo-soo]
main road a rua principal [roo-uh preen-sipal]
  (*in the country*) a estrada principal
  [shtrah-duh ...]
man um homem [ommeng]

manager o gerente [jerent]
map um mapa [mah-puh]
market o mercado [merkah-doo]
match: a box of matches uma caixa de fósforos [kye-shuh duh fosh-fooroosh]
matter: it doesn't matter não faz mal [nowng fash mal]
maybe talvez [tal-vesh]
me: for me para mim [para meeng]
  with me comigo [koomeegoo]
mean: what does this mean? o que significa isto? [oo kuh seegnifeekuh eeshtoo]
menu a ementa [eementuh]
milk o leite [layt]
mineral water água mineral [ahg-wuh meen-ral]
minute um minuto [meenootoo]
Monday segunda-feira [segoonduh fay-ruh]
money dinheiro [din-yay-roo]
more mais [my-sh]
  more wine, please um pouco mais de vinho, por favor [oom po-koo my-sh duh veen-yoo ...]
morning a manhã [man-yang]
  good morning bom dia [bong dee-uh]
mother: my mother minha mãe [meen-yuh my-ng]
motorbike uma mota [mottuh]
motorway a auto-estrada [owtoo-shtrah-duh]
mountain uma montanha [montahn-yuh]
much muito [mweentoo]
  not much não muito [nowng ...]
music a música [moozickuh]
must: I must ... tenho de ... [ten-yoo duh]
  I must not eat ... não devo comer ... [nowng devvoo koomair]
my o meu/a minha [oo meh-oo/uh meen-yuh]
name o nome [nom]
  my name is ... chamo-me ... [shah-moo-muh]
  what's your name? como se chama? [ko-moo suh shah-muh]

near: is it near? fica perto? [*feekuh pairtoo*]
  near here aqui perto [*akee ...*]
necessary necessário [*nussussaree-oo*]
needle uma agulha [*agool-yuh*]
never nunca [*noonkuh*]
new novo/nova [*no-voo/novvuh*]
newspaper um jornal [*joornal*]
next próximo [*prossimoo*]
nice agradável [*agradah-vel*]
night a noite [*noyt*]
  good night boa noite [*bo-uh noyt*]
no não [*nowng*]
  there's no water não há água [*nowng ah ahg-wuh*]
nobody ninguém [*neen-gayng*]
noisy barulhento [*barool-yentoo*]
not não [*nowng*]
  not me eu não [*eh-oo nowng*]
  not that one esse não [*ehss nowng*]
nothing nada [*nah-duh*]
now agora [*a-goruh*]
nowhere em parte nenhuma [*eng part nun-yoomuh*]
number o número [*noomeroo*]
of de [*duh*]
often muitas vezes [*mweentush veh-zush*]
oil óleo [*ollee-oo*]
OK O.K.
old velho [*vel-yoo*]
on em [*eng*]
one um/uma [*oom/oomuh*]
only: only one só um/uma [*so oom/oomuh*]
open aberto [*a-bair-too*]
or ou [*oh*]
orange juice sumo de laranja [*soo-moo duh larahn-juh*]
other: the other one o outro [*oo oh-troo*]
our nosso [*nossoo*]/nossa [*nossuh*]
over: over here/there cá/lá [*kah/lah*]
pain uma dor

painkillers calmantes [kalmantsh]
paper papel [puppel]
pardon? como disse? [ko-moo deess]
passport o passaporte [pass-port]
pen uma caneta [kanettuh]
people a gente [jent]
petrol a gasolina [gazooleenuh]
photograph uma fotografia [footoografee-uh]
piece um pedaço [pedah-soo]
plane um avião [uh-vee-owng]
platform: which platform? qual é o cais [kwal eh oo kye-sh]
please por favor [poor fuh-vor]
police a polícia [pooleess-yuh]
pool (*swimming*) uma piscina [peesh-seenuh]
Portugal Portugal [poortoogal]
Portuguese português [poortoogesh]
possible possível [poo-seevel]
postcard um postal [pooshtal]
post office o correio [koorayoo]
pretty bonito [booneetoo]
problem um problema [proobleh-muh]
pronounce: how do you pronounce it? como se pronuncia? [ko-moo suh proonoon-see-uh]
purse uma bolsa [bole-suh]
quiet tranquilo [tran-kweeloo]
quite (*fairly*) bastante [bushtant]
rain: it's raining está a chover [shtah shoovair]
ready: when will it be ready? quando está pronto? [kwandoo shtah pront]
receipt um recibo [reseeboo]
red vermelho [vermel-yoo]
rent: can I rent a car? posso alugar um carro? [possoo aloogar oom karroo]
repair: can you repair it? pode consertá-lo [pod konsertah-loo]
reservation uma reserva [rezairvuh]
restaurant um restaurante [rushtoh-rant]
return: a return to ... uma ida e volta para ... [oomuh eeduh ee voltuh para]

....

right: on the right à direita [ah deer*ay*tuh]
   that's right está certo [shtah *sai*rtoo]
river um rio [*ree*-oo]
road a estrada [shtr*ah*-duh]
room um quarto [kw*a*rtoo]
   have you got a (single/double) room? tem
   um quarto (individual/de casal)? [teng oom
   kw*a*rtoo (eendivid-w*a*l/duh kaz*a*l)]
   for one/three night(s) para uma noite/três
   noites [para *oo*muh noyt/tresh noytsh]
safe seguro [seg*oo*roo]
salt o sal [sal]
same mesmo [m*e*jmoo]
Saturday sábado [s*a*b-doo]
say: how do you say ... in Portuguese? como se
   diz ... em português? [k*o*-moo suh deesh ... eng
   poortoo-gh*e*sh]
   what did he say? o que é que ele disse? [oo kee
   eh kehl deess]
scissors uma tesoura [tez*o*h-ruh]
Scotland Escócia [shk*o*ss-yuh]
sea o mar
seat um assento [ass*e*ntoo]
see ver [vair]
   oh, I see já percebo [jah pers*e*bboo]
send mand*a*r
shampoo um champô [shamp*o*h]
she ela [*e*lluh]; **is she ...?** é ...? [eh]
shirt uma camisa [kam*ee*zuh]
shoes sapatos [sap*a*h-toosh]
shop uma loja [l*o*jjuh]
show: please show me pode mostrar-me, por
   favor? [pod moosh-tr*a*rmuh, poor fuh-v*o*r]
shower: with shower com duche [kong doosh]
shut fechado [fesh*a*h-doo]
single: a single to ... uma ida para ... [*oo*muh
   *ee*duh para]
sister irmã [eer-m*a*ng]
sit: can I sit here? posso sentar-me aqui? [*po*ssoo
   sent*a*r-muh ak*ee*]

skirt uma saia [sa-yuh]
slow lento [lentoo]
small pequeno [pickeh-noo]
so tanto [tantoo]
  not so much não tanto [nowng ...]
soap o sabonete [saboonet]
somebody alguém [al-gheng]
something alguma coisa [algoomuh koy-zuh]
son: my son meu filho [meh-oo feel-yoo]
soon cedo [seh-doo]
sorry: (I'm) sorry desculpe [dushkoolp]
souvenir uma lembrança [lembran-suh]
speak: do you speak English? fala inglês?
  [fah-luh eenglesh]
  I don't speak Portuguese não falo português
  [nowng fah-loo poortoo-ghesh]
spoon uma colher [kool-yair]
stairs a escada [shkah-duh]
stamp um selo [selloo]
  two stamps for England dois selos para
  Inglaterra [doysh selloosh para eenglaterruh]
station a estação [shtassowng]
sticking plaster um adesivo [ad-zeevoo]
stolen: my wallet's been stolen roubaram-me a
  carteira [ro-barowng-muh uh kartayruh]
stop! pare! [par]
street a rua [roo-uh]
strong forte [fort]
student um estudante [shtoodant]
sugar açúcar [assookar]
suitcase uma mala [mah-luh]
sun o sol
sunburn queimadura de sol [kay-madooruh ...]
Sunday domingo [doomeengoo]
sunglasses óculos de sol [okkooloosh ...]
sunshade uma pára-sol [paruh-sol]
sunstroke uma insolação [eensooluh-sowng]
suntan oil óleo para bronzear [ollee-oo ...]
swim: I'm going for a swim vou tomar banho
  [voh toomar bahn-yoo]

....

table: a table for 4 uma mesa para quatro
   pessoas [meh-zuh para kwatroo pussoh-ush]
taxi um táxi
tea chá [sha]
telegram um telegrama [tulluh-grah-muh]
telephone o telefone [tulluh-fon]
   UK is 0744 and drop first 0 of area code
tent uma tenda [tenduh]
terrible terrível [terreevel]
thank you (*men say*) obrigado
   (*women say*) obrigada [o-breegah-doo/duh]
   YOU MAY THEN HEAR
   não tem de quê *you're welcome*
   no thank you não obrigado/a [nowng ...]
that: that man esse homem [ehss ommeng]
   that (one) isso [ee-soo]
the o/a [oo, uh]; (*plural*) os/as [oosh, ush]
them: for them para eles [par eh-lush]
there ali [alee]
   is there .../are there ...? há ...?
these estes/estas [eh-shtush/eshtush]
they eles/elas [eh-lush/ellush]
   are they ...? são ...? [sowng]
thirsty: I'm thirsty tenho sede [tenyoo sed]
this: this hotel este hotel [ehsht o-tel]
   is this ...? é isto ...? [eh eeshtoo]
those esses/essas [eh-sush/essush]
Thursday quinta-feira [keentuh fayruh]
ticket um bilhete [oom beel-yet]
time tempo [tempoo]; *see pages 124–125*
tired cansado [kansah-doo]
tissues lenços de papel [lensoosh duh puppell]
to: to Lisbon/England a Lisboa/para Inglaterra
   [uh leej-bo-uh/para eengluh-terruh]
today hoje [oje]
together junto [joontoo]
toilet o quarto de banho [kwartoo duh bahn-yoo]
tomorrow amanhã [aman-yang]
   the day after tomorrow depois de amanhã
   [duh-poysh daman-yang]

tonight esta noite [eshtuh noyt]
too demasiado [demuz-yah-doo]
   (*also*) também [tambeng]
   that's too much é demasiado [eh ...]
tour uma excursão [shkoorsowng]
tourist um turista [tooreeshtuh]
tourist office o turismo [tooreej-moo]
towel uma toalha [too-al-yuh]
town uma cidade [seedahd]
   (*small*) uma vila [veeluh]
train o comboio [komboyyoo]
translate traduzir [tradoozeer]
travel agency a agência de viagens [ajenss-yuh
   duh vee-ah-jensh]
trousers as calças [ush kal-sush]
try tentar
Tuesday terça-feira [tersuh-fayruh]
understand: I don't understand não percebo
   [nowng persebboo]
urgent urgente [oor-jent]
us: for us para nós [para nosh]
   with us connosco [konoshkoo]
use: can I use ...? posso usar ...? [possoo oozar]
vegetarian vegetariano [vejeturry-ah-noo]
very muito [mweentoo]
   very much imenso [eemensoo]
village uma aldeia [al-day-uh]
wait: I'm waiting for a friend estou à espera
   dum amigo [shtoh ah shpairuh doom ameegoo]
wake: will you wake me up at 7.30? pode
   acordar-me às sete e meia? [pod akoordar-muh
   ash set ee mayyuh]
Wales País de Gales [pa-eesh duh gah-lush]
want: I want a ... queria um ... [kree-uh oom]
   I don't want to não quero [nowng kairoo]
warm quente [kent]
water água [ahg-wuh]
we nós [nosh]; **we are ...** somos [so-moosh]
Wednesday quarta-feira [kwarta fayruh]
week uma semana [semah-nuh]

....

well: how are you? – very well, thanks como
está? – muito bem, obrigado [ko-moo shtah –
mweentoo beng, o-breegah-doo]
wet molhado [mol-yah-doo]
what? o quê? [oo keh]
  what is that? o que é isso? [oo kee eh eessoo]
when? quando? [kwandoo]
where? onde? [ond]
  where is ...? onde é ...? [ondee eh]
which? qual? [kwal]
white branco [brankoo]
who? quem? [keng]
why? porquê? [poor-keh]
  why not? porque não? [poorkuh nowng]
wife: my wife minha mulher [meen-yuh
mool-yair]
window a janela [janelluh]
wine vinho [veen-yoo]
with com [kong]
without sem [seng]
woman uma mulher [mool-yair]
work: it's not working não funciona [nowng
foonss-yonnuh]
write: could you write it down? pode escrever
isso? [pod shkruvvair eesoo]
wrong errado [eerah-doo]
  what's wrong? o que aconteceu? [oo kee
akontusseh-oo]
year um ano [ah-noo]
yes sim [seeng]
yesterday ontem [onteng]
you (to a man) o senhor; (to a woman) a senhora
[oo sun-yor/uh sun-yoruh]
  (to people you know well) você [vo-seh]
  with you consigo [konseegoo]
  are you ...? (o senhor/a senhora) é ...? [eh]
young jovem [jovveng]
your o seu/a sua [seh-oo/soo-uh]
youth hostel albergue da juventude [albairg duh
jooventood]

....

0	zero [zairoo]		
1	um [oom]	**11**	onze [onz]
2	dois [doysh]	**12**	doze [dohz]
3	três [tresh]	**13**	treze [traiz]
4	quatro [kwatroo]	**14**	catorze [katorz]
5	cinco [seenkoo]	**15**	quinze [keenz]
6	seis [saysh]	**16**	dezasseis [duzzasaysh]
7	sete [set]	**17**	dezasete [duzzaset]
8	oito [oytoo]	**18**	dezoito [duz-oy-too]
9	nove [nov]	**19**	dezanove [duzzanov]
10	dez [desh]	**20**	vinte [veent]

21 vinte e um [veent-ee-oom]
22 vinte e dois [veent-ee-doysh]
30 trinta [treentuh]
31 trinta e um [treent-ee-oom]
40 quarenta [kwarentuh]
50 cinquenta [seenkwentuh]
60 sessenta [sessentuh]
70 setenta [setentuh]
80 oitenta [oy-tentuh]
90 noventa [nooventuh]
100 cem [seng]
101 cento e um [sentoo-ee-oom]
·**165** cento e sessenta e cinco
  [sentoo-ee-sessent-ee-seenkoo]
200 duzentos [doozentoosh]
300 trezentos [trezentoosh]
400 quatrocentos [kwatroo-sentoosh]
500 quinhentos [keen-yentoosh]
600 seiscentos [saysh-sentoosh]
700 setecentos [set-sentoosh]
800 oitocentos [oy-toosentoosh]
900 novecentos [nov-sentoosh]
1,000 mil [meel]
2,000 dois mil [doysh meel]
4,650 quatro mil seiscentos e cinquenta
1,000,000 um milhão [oom meel-yowng]

for thousands use a full-stop: 3.000
for decimals use a comma: 4,6 [... veergooluh ...]

....

ENTRADAS: Starters
cocktail de gambas *prawn cocktail*
salada de atum *tuna salad*
melão *melon*
sumo de laranja/tomate *orange/tomato juice*
chouriço *smoked pork sausage*
ovos à Minhota *baked eggs, tomato, onions*
omeleta de marisco *shellfish omelette*
omeleta de presunto/cogumelos *cured
    ham/mushroom omelette*

SOPA: Soup
açorda de alho *bread soup, garlic, herbs*
canja *chicken broth and rice*
caldo verde *potato broth, shredded cabbage*
gaspacho *refreshing cold soup: tomatoes, green
    peppers and cucumber*

PEIXE: Fish dishes
ameijoas *clams*
gambas *scampi*
santola *crab*
sardinhas assadas *charcoal-grilled sardines*
salmão grelhado *grilled salmon*
bacalhau à Gomes de Sá *cod baked with parsley,
    potatoes, onion, olives etc*
chocos *cuttlefish*
lulas/calamares *squid*
lampreia *lamprey*
caldeirada *mixed fish in onions, potato*

CARNE: Meat dishes
carne de vaca (assada) *(roast) beef*
borrego *lamb*
porco *pork*
frango *chicken*
vitela *veal*
um bife de ... a ... *steak*
costeleta *cutlet/chop*
leitão *suckling pig*

cordorniz *quail*
faisão *pheasant*
peru *turkey*
cozido à Portuguesa *boiled beef, gammon, smoked sausage, rice and vegetables*
arroz de frango *fried chicken in wine, ham and rice casserole*
frango na púcara *chicken stewed in Port and brandy, fried with almonds*
almôndegas *meatballs*
espetada mista *shish-kebab*
feijoada *pigs feet, sausage, white beans and cabbage*

SOBREMESA: Dessert
Fruit: ananás *pineapple*
        melancia *watermelon*
        cerejas *cherries*
        ameixas *plums*
        morangos *strawberries*

Sweets: salada de frutas *fruit cocktail*
        pudim flã *crème caramel*
        pudim molotov *eggwhite mousse, caramel*
        arroz doce *rice pudding*
        farófias *eggwhite beaten with milk, egg custard and cinnamon*
        gelado *ice cream*

Cheese: queijo de Elvas *mild white*
        queijo de azeitão *matured in oil*
        queijo fresco *very bland goat's milk cheese*

COFFEE: *most Portuguese have a small strong black coffee after a meal called 'uma bica' [beekuh]; if you prefer it weaker, ask for a 'carioca'; the equivalent to our white coffee is a 'galão' [galowng] – this is a large cup; for a smaller white coffee, ask for 'um garoto'*

GREEK

Special sounds in the pronunciation guide:

th	is like th in 'theatre' as against th in 'there'
kh	is like the ch in Scottish 'loch'
e	is pronounced as in 'wet'
o	is pronounced as in 'hot'

Letters printed in italics show which part of a word should be stressed.

kalo taxeethee!
[καλό ταξίδι]
have a good trip!

a, an enas, meea, ena [ένας, μία, ένα]
accident ena theesteekheema [ένα δυστύχημα]
adaptor ena polaplo [ένα πολλαπλό]
address ee thee-ef-theensee [η διεύθυνση]
after: after you meta apo sas [μετά από σας]
afternoon to apo-yevma [το απόγευμα]
 good afternoon kaleespera [καλησπέρα]
again xana [ξανά]
airport to a-erothromeeo [το αεροδρόμιο]
all ola [όλα]
 all right endaxee [εντάξει]
almost skhethon [σχεδόν]
alone monos [μόνος]
always panda [πάντα]
and ke [και]
another: another room ena alo thomateeo [ένα
 άλλο δωμάτιο]
 another beer, please alee meea beera
 parakalo [άλλη μία μπύρα, παρακαλώ]
arrive fthano [φθάνω]
ashtray ena tassakee [ένα τασάκι]
ask roto [ρωτώ]
baby to moro [το μωρό]
back: I'll be right back tha yeereesso greegora
 [θα γυρίσω γρήγορα]
bad as-kheema [άσχημα]
bag ee tsanda [η τσάντα]
 (suitcase) ee valeetsa [η βαλίτσα]
bank ee trapeza [η τράπεζα]
bar to bar [το μπαρ]
bath to baneeo [το μπάνιο]
bathroom to lootro [το λουτρό]
beach ee paraleea [η παραλία]
beautiful oreos [ωραίος]
because epeethee [επειδή]
bed to krevatee [το κρεβάτι]
beer meea beera [μιά μπύρα]
before preen [πριν]
best kaleeteros [καλύτερος]
better kaleetera [καλύτερα]

bicycle ena potheelato [ένα ποδήλατο]
big megalo [μεγάλο]
bill o logareeazmos [ο λογαριασμός]
black mavro [μαύρο]
blanket ee kooverta [η κουβέρτα]
blue ble [μπλε]
boat to pleeo [το πλοίο]
book to veevleeo [το βιβλίο]
boring aneearos [ανιαρός]
both ke ee theeo [και οι δύο]
bottle ena bookalee [ένα μπουκάλι]
boy to agoree [το αγόρι]
brakes ta frena [τα φρένα]
bread to psomee [το ψωμί]
breakfast to pro-yevma [το πρόγευμα]
broken spazmeno [σπασμένο]
brother: my brother o athelfos moo [ο αδελφός
   μου]
bus to leoforeeo [το λεωφορείο]
bus stop ee stassee [η στάση]
butter vooteero [βούτυρο]
café to zakharoplasteeo [το ζαχαροπλαστείο]
camera ee fotografeekee meekhanee
   [η φωτογραφική μηχανή]
campsite 'camping' [κάμπινγκ]
can: can I have ...? boro na ekho ...?
   [μπορώ να έχω ...;]
   can you ...? boreete ...? [μπορείτε ...;]
   I can't ... then boro ... [δεν μπορώ]
cancel: I want to cancel ... thelo na akeerosso ...
   [θέλω να ακυρώσω ...]
car to aftokeeneeto [το αυτοκίνητο]
car park to parking [το πάρκινγκ]
centre to kendro [το κέντρο]
change: can you change this into drachmas?
   boreete na moo alaxete afto se thrakhmes?
   [μπορείτε να μου αλλάξετε αυτό σε δραχμές;]
   I'd like to change my reservation tha eethela
   na alaxo teen krateessee [θα ήθελα να αλλάξω
   την κράτηση]

....

cheap *ftheenos* [φθηνός]
cheers! steen eeyeea soo [στην υγειά σου]
cheese to teer*ee* [το τυρί]
chemist's to farmak*eeo* [το φαρμακείο]
cheque *ena* tsek [ένα τσεκ]
children ta peth*eea* [τα παιδιά]
chips patates teeganeetes [πατάτες τηγανητές]
church ee ekleess*eea* [η εκκλησία]
cigar *ena* pooro [ένα πούρο]
cigarette *ena* tseegaro [ένα τσιγάρο]
clean ka*th*aros [καθαρός]
clothes ta rookha [τα ρούχα]
coffee *ena* kafe [ένα καφέ]
   a white coffee *ena* kafe me gala [ένα καφέ με
   γάλα]
cold kreeo [κρύο]
comb ee khtena [η χτένα]
come erkhome [έρχομαι]
   come in! ela [έλα]
constipation theeskeeleeotees [δυσκοιλιότης]
consul o proxenos [ο Πρόξενος]
cost: what does it cost? posso kanee? [πόσο
   κάνει;]
could: could you please ...? *th*a boroossate ...?
   [θα μπορούσατε ...;]
   could I have ...? boro na ekho ...? [μπορώ να
   έχω ...;]
crazy trelos [τρελλός]
crisps tseeps [τσίπς]
Customs to teloneeo [το τελωνείο]
dark skoteenos [σκοτεινός]
daughter: my daughter ee koreemoo [η κόρη μου]
delicious yefstee-kotatos [γευστικώτατος]
dentist othondee-atros [οδοντίατρος]
develop: could you develop these? boreete na
   tees emfaneessete? [μπορείτε να τις
   εμφανίσετε;]
different: a different room *ena* alo thomateeo
   [ένα άλλο δωμάτιο;]
difficult *th*eeskolos [δύσκολος]

dinner to theepno [το δείπνο]
do: how do you do? khero polee [χαίρω πολύ]
doctor o yatros [ο γιατρός]
door ee porta [η πόρτα]
dress to foostanee [το φουστάνι]
drink ena poto [ένα ποτό]
driving licence atheea otheeyeesseos [άδεια οδηγήσεως]
drunk metheezmenos [μεθυσμένος]
dry cleaner stegnokathareestee-reeo [στεγνοκαθαριστήριο]
early norees [νωρίς]
easy efkolos [εύκολος]
eat: something to eat katee na fa-o [κάτι να φάω]
else: something else katee alo [κάτι άλλο]
England Angleea [Αγγλία]
English (*language*) Angleeka [Αγγλικά]
enough: that's enough ftanee [φτάνει]
entertainment ee theeaskethassee [η διασκέδαση]
evening to theeleeno [το δειλινό]
  good evening kaleespera [καλησπέρα]
everyone kathenas [καθένας]
everything ola [όλα]
excellent exokhos [έξοχος]
excuse me me seenkhoreete [με συγχωρείτε]
  (*to get attention*) sas parakalo [σας παρακαλώ]
expensive akreevo [ακριβό]
far: is it far? eene makreea? [είναι μακρυά;]
fast greegora [γρήγορα]
  don't speak so fast mee meelas tosso greegora [μη μιλάς τόσο γρήγορα]
father: my father o pateras moo [ο πατέρας μου]
ferry to ferry-boat [το φέρρυμποτ]
few: only a few mono leeyee [μόνο λίγοι]
film to film [το φιλμ]
first protos [πρώτος]
food to fayeeto [το φαγητό]
for ya [για]
fork ena peeroonee [ένα πηρούνι]

free ele*th*eros [ελεύθερος]
Friday Paraskev*ee* [Παρασκευή]
friend o f*ee*los [ο φίλος]
from apo [από]
fun: it's fun *ee*ne theeaskethasteek*o* [είναι διασκεδαστικό]
funny (*strange*) peree-ergo [περίεργο]
(*comical*) asteeo [αστείο]
garage (*repair*) to seener-yeeo [το συνεργείο]
(*parking*) to garaz [το γκαράζ]
girl ena koreetsee [ένα κορίτσι]
give theeno [δίνω]
glasses ta yalee*a* [τα γυαλιά]
go: it's/he's gone efeeye [έφυγε]
   I want tc **go to Delphi** *the*lo na pao stoos Thelfoos [θέλω να πάω στους Δελφούς]
good kala [καλά]
goodbye *y*assoo [γειά σου]
Greece Elatha [Ελλάδα]
Greek *E*leenas ['Ελληνας]
guide o ksenagos [ο ξεναγός]
hairdresser's ee komotria [η κομμώτρια]
handbag ee tsanda [η τσάντα]
happy efteekheezmenos [ευτυχισμένος]
harbour to leemanee [το λιμάνι]
hard skleeros [σκληρός]
(*difficult*) theeskolos [δύσκολος]
have ekho [έχω]
   I (don't) have ... (then) ekho ... [(δεν) έχω]
   do you have ...? ekhete ...? [έχετε ...;]
he aftos [αυτός]; **is he ...?** *ee*ne ...? [είναι ...;]
headache ponokefalos [πονοκέφαλος]
hello *y*assoo [γειά σου]
help: can you help? boreete na me voee*th*eessete? [μπορείτε να με βοηθήσετε;]
her aftee [αυτή]
   with her mazee tees [μαζί της]
   it's her bag *ee*ne ee tsanda tees [είναι η τσάντα της]
here etho [εδώ]

him afton [αυτόν]
   with him maz*ee* too [μαζί του]
his: it's his drink, it's his *ee*ne to pot*o* too, *ee*ne
   theek*o* too [είναι το ποτό του, είναι δικό του]
holiday theeak*o*pes [διακοπές]
home: at home sto speet*ee* [στο σπίτι]
hospital to nossokom*ee*o [το νοσοκομείο]
hot zest*o* [ζεστό]
hotel to ksenothokh*ee*o [το ξενοδοχείο]
hour ee or*a* [η ώρα]
house to speet*ee* [το σπίτι]
how? pos? [πώς;]
   how many? poss*ee*? [πόσοι;]
   how much? poss*a*? [πόσα;]
   how are you? tee kan*ee*s? [τί κάνεις;]
hungry: I'm hungry/not hungry peen*a*o/then
   peen*a*o [πεινάω/δεν πεινάω]
hurt: it hurts pon*a*ee [πονάει]
husband: my husband o s*ee*zeegos moo
   [ο σύζυγός μου]
I ego [εγώ]; **I am ...** *ee*me ... [είμαι ...]
ice o pag*o*s [ο πάγος]
ice cream ena pagot*o* [ένα παγωτό]
if an [αν]
ill *a*rostos [άρρωστος]
immediately am*e*ssos [αμέσως]
important spoothe*o*s [σπουδαίος]
in sto [στο]
insect repellent endomokt*o*no [εντομοκτόνο]
Ireland Eerlanth*ee*a [Ιρλανδία]
it aft*o* [αυτό]; **is it ...?** *ee*ne ...? [είναι ...;]
jacket to sak*a*ki [το σακάκι]
just: just two mono th*ee*o [μόνο δύο]
key to kleeth*ee* [το κλειδί]
kiss ena feel*ee* [ένα φιλί]
knife ena makher*ee* [ένα μαχαίρι]
know: I don't know then ks*e*ro [δεν ξέρω]
last telefte*o*s [τελευταίος]
   last night kh-*the*s vrath*ee* [χθες βράδυ]
late arg*a* [αργά]

later argotera [αργότερα]
   see you later *th*a se tho argotera [θα σε δω αργότερα]
leave: we're leaving tomorrow fevgoome avreeo [φεύγουμε αύριο]
   when does the bus leave? pote fevgee to leoforeeo? [πότε φεύγει το λεωφορείο;]
   I left two shirts in my room afeessa theeo pookameessa sto thomateeo moo [άφησα δύο πουκάμισα στο δωμάτιό μου]
   can I leave this here? boro nafeesso afto etho? [μπορώ ν'αφήσω αυτό εδώ;]
left: on the left pros tareestera [προς τ' αριστερά]
left luggage o khoros felaxeos aposkevon [ο χώρος φυλάξεως αποσκευών]
letter to grama [το γράμμα]
light to fos [το φως]
   do you have a light? ekhete foteea? [έχετε φωτιά;]
like: would you like ...? *th*a *th*elate ...? [θα θέλατε …;]
   I'd like a .../I'd like to ... *th*a eethela ena .../tha eethela na ... [θα ήθελα ένα …/θα ήθελα να …]
   I like it moo aressee [μου αρέσει]
   I don't like it then moo aressee [δεν μου αρέσει]
little meekros [μικρός]
   a little leego [λίγο]
lorry to forteego [το φορτηγό]
lose: I've lost ... ekhassa ... [έχασα …]
   I'm lost ekho kha*th*ee [έχω χαθεί]
lot: a lot/not a lot pola/okhee pola [πολλά/όχι πολλά]
luggage ee aposkeves [οι αποσκευές]
lunch to yevma [το γεύμα]
main road o kendreekos thromos [ο κεντρικός δρόμος]
man o anthras [ο άνδρας]
manager o theeakheereestees [ο διαχειριστής]
map o khartees [ο χάρτης]
market, marketplace ee agora [η αγορά]

....

match: a box of matches ena kootee speerta [ένα
κουτί σπίρτα]
matter: it doesn't matter then peerazee [δεν
πειράζει]
maybe boree [μπορεί]
me ego [εγώ]
mean: what does this mean? tee enoee afto? [τί
εννοεί αυτό;]
menu katalogos fayeeton [κατάλογος φαγητών]
milk gala [γάλα]
mineral water metaleeko nero [μεταλλικό νερό]
minute ena lepto [ένα λεπτό]
Monday Theftera [Δευτέρα]
money lefta [λεφτά]
more pereessotero [περισσότερο]
  may I have some more? boro na ekho akomee
  leego? [μπορώ να έχω ακόμη λίγο;]
  more wine, please kee alo krassee parakalo
  [κι άλλο κρασί, παρακαλώ]
morning to proee [το πρωί]
  good morning kaleemera [καλημέρα]
mother: my mother ee meetera moo [η μητέρα
μου]
motorbike ee motosseekleta [η μοτοσυκλέτα]
mountain to voono [το βουνό]
much polee [πολύ]
  not much [όχι πολύ]
music moosseekee [μουσική]
must: I must ... prepee na ... [πρέπει να ...]
  I must not eat ... then prepee na fa-o ... [δεν
  πρέπει να φάω ...]
  you must prepee [πρέπει]
my: my hotel to ksenothokheeo moo
[το ξενοδοχείο μου]
name to onoma [το όνομα]
  my name is ... me lene ... [με λένε ...]
  what's your name? pos se lene? [πως σε λένε;]
near: is it near? eene konda? [είναι κοντά;]
necessary anangeo [αναγκαίο]
needle meea velona [μιά βελόνα]

never pote [ποτέ]
newspaper ee efeem*ee*tha [η εφημερίδα]
next epomenos [επόμενος]
nice kalo [καλό]
night vrathee [βράδυ]
    good night kaleen*ee*kta [καληνύκτα]
no okhee [όχι]
    there's no ... then ekhee ... [δεν έχει ...]
nobody kanenas [κανένας]
noisy thoreevothees [θορυβώδης]
not then [δεν]
    not me/that okhee ego/afto [όχι εγώ/αυτό]
nothing teepote [τίποτε]
now tora [τώρα]
nowhere poothena [πουθενά]
number o areethmos [ο αριθμός]
of too [του]
often seekhna [συχνά]
oil lathee [λάδι]
OK endaxee [εντάξει]
old yeros [γέρος]
on pano [πάνω]
one enas [ένας]
only mono [μόνο]
open aneekta [ανοικτά]
or ee [ή]
orange juice kheemos portokaleeoo [χυμός
    πορτοκαλιού]
other: the other one to alo [το άλλο]
our: our hotel to ksenothokheeo mas
    [το ξενοδοχείο μας]
over: over here/there etho/ekee [εδώ/εκεί]
pain o ponos [ο πόνος]
painkiller ena pafseepono [ένα παυσίπονο]
paper khartee [χαρτί]
pardon? seegnomee? [συγγνώμη;]
passport to theeavateereeo [το διαβατήριο]
pen ena steelo [ένα στυλό]
people anthropee [άνθρωποι]
petrol ee venzeenee [η βενζίνη]

photograph meea fotografeea [μιά φωτογραφία]
piece ena komatee [ένα κομμάτι]
plane to a-eroplano [το αεροπλάνο]
platform: which platform? peea platforma?
[ποιά πλατφόρμα;]
please parakalo [παρακαλώ]
police ee asteenomeea [η αστυνομία]
pool (*swimming*) ee peesseena [η πισίνα]
possible peethano [πιθανό]
postcard ee karta [η κάρτα]
post office to takheethromeeo [το ταχυδρομείο]
pretty orea [ωραία]
problem ena provleema [ένα πρόβλημα]
pronounce: how do you pronounce this? pos
to proferees afto? [πώς το προφέρεις αυτό;]
purse to portofolee [το πορτοφόλι]
quiet eesseekha [ήσυχα]
quite (*fairly*) arketa [αρκετά]
rain: it's raining vrekhee [βρέχει]
ready: when will it be ready? pote tha eene
eteemo? [πότε θα είναι έτοιμο;]
receipt meea apotheexee [μία απόδειξη]
red kokkeeno [κόκκινο]
rent: can I rent ...? boro na neekeeasso ...? [μπορώ
να νοικιάσω;]
repair: can you repair it? boreete na to
epeeskevassete? [μπορείτε να το επισκευάσετε;]
reservation krateessee thesseos [κράτηση θέσεως]
restaurant to esteeatoreeo [το εστιατόριο]
return: a return to ... ena eesseeteereeo
metepeestrofees ya ... [ένα εισιτήριο
μετ'επιστροφής γιά ...]
right: that's right sosta [σωστά]
on the right sta thexeea [στα δεξιά]
river to potamee [το ποτάμι]
road o thromos [ο δρόμος]
room to thomateeo [το δωμάτιο]
do you have a (single/double) room? ekhete
ena mono/theeplo thomateeo? [έχετε ένα
μονό/διπλό δωμάτιο;]

for one night/for three nights ya meea vratheea/ya trees vrathee-es [γιά μιά βραδιά/γιά τρεις βραδιές]

safe asfales [ασφαλές]

salt to alatee [το αλάτι]

same eetheeos [ίδιος]

Saturday Savato [Σάββατο]

say: how do you say ... in Greek? pos lene ... sta eleeneeka? [πώς λένε ... στα Ελληνικά;]

what did he say? tee eere? [τί είπε;]

scissors ena psaleethee [ένα ψαλίδι]

Scotland Skoteea [Σκωτία]

sea ee thalassa [η θάλασσα]

seat meea thessee [μιά θέση]

see vlepo [βλέπω]

oh, I see ah, katalava [α, κατάλαβα]

can I see the room? boro na tho to thomateeo? [μπορώ να δω το δωμάτιο;]

send stelno [στέλνω]

shampoo ena sampooan [ένα σαμπουάν]

she aftee [αυτή]; **is she ...?** eene ...? [είναι ...;]

shirt to pookameesso [το πουκάμισο]

shoes papootseea [παπούτσια]

shop to magazee [το μαγαζί]

show: please show me parakalo theexe moo [παρακαλώ, δείξε μου]

shower: with shower me doos [με ντους]

shut: it was shut eetan kleesto [ήταν κλειστό]

single: a single to ... ena mono eesseeteereeo ya ... [ένα μονό εισιτήριο γιά ...]

sister: my sister ee athelfee moo [η αδελφή μου]

sit: can I sit here? boro na katso etho? [μπορώ να κάτσω εδώ;]

skirt ee foosta [η φούστα]

slow arga [αργά]

small meekro [μικρό]

so: not so much okhee tosso polee [όχι τόσο πολύ]

soap ena sapoonee [ένα σαπούνι]

somebody kapeeos [κάποιος]

....

something katee [κάτι]
son: my son o yeeos moo [ο γιός μου]
soon seendoma [σύντομα]
sorry: (I'm) sorry leepame [λυπάμαι]
souvenir ena entheemeeo [ένα ενθύμιο]
speak: do you speak English? meelate
  Agleeka? [μιλάτε Αγγλικά;]
  I don't speak Greek then meelo Eleeneeka
  [δεν μιλώ Ελληνικά]
spoon ena kootalee [ένα κουτάλι]
stairs ee skales [οι σκάλες]
stamp ena grammatosseemo [ένα γραμματόσημο]
  two stamps for England theeo
  grammatosseema ya teen Angleea [δύο
  γραμματόσημα γιά την Αγγλία]
station o stathmos [ο σταθμός]
sticking plaster lefkoplast [λευκοπλάστ]
stolen: my wallet's been stolen moo klepsane to
  portofolee [μού κλέψανε το πορτοφόλι]
stop! stamata [σταμάτα]
street o thromos [ο δρόμος]
strong theenatos [δυνατός]
student feeteetees [φοιτητής]
sugar ee zakharee [η ζάχαρη]
suitcase ee valeetsa [η βαλίτσα]
sun o eeleeos [ο ήλιος]
sunburn kamenos apo ton eeleeo [καμμένος από
  τον ήλιο]
Sunday Keereeakee [Κυριακή]
sunglasses yaleea eeleeoo [γυαλιά ηλίου]
sunshade ee ombrela [η ομπρέλα]
sunstroke eeleeassee [ηλίαση]
suntan oil lathee eeleeoo [λάδι ηλίου]
swim: I'm going for a swim pao ya koleembee
  [πάω γιά κολύμπι]
table: a table for 4 ena trapezee ya tesserees [ένα
  τραπέζι γιά τέσσερις]
taxi ena taxee [ένα ταξί]
tea tsaee [τσάι]
telegram ena teelegrafeema [ένα τηλεγράφημα]

....

telephone to teelefono [το τηλέφωνο]
  UK is 0044 and drop first 0 of area code
tent ee tenda [η τέντα]
terrible fovero [φοβερό]
thank you efkhareesto [ευχαριστώ]
  YOU MAY THEN HEAR ...
  parakalo *you're welcome*
  no thank you okhee efkhareesto [όχι ...]
that ekeeno [εκείνο]
  that table ekeeno to trapezee [εκείνο το τραπέζι]
  that one ekeeno [εκείνο]
the o, ee, to [ο, η, το]; *(plural)* ee, ee, ta [οι, οι, τα]
them: with them mazee toos [μαζί τους]
there ekee [εκεί]
  is there/are there ...? eeparkhee .../
  eeparkhoon ...? [υπάρχει .../υπάρχουν ...;]
these aftee, aftes, afta [αυτοί, αυτές, αυτά]
they aftee, aftes, afta [αυτοί, αυτές, αυτά]
  are they ...? eene ...? [είναι ...;]
thirsty: I'm thirsty theepso [διψώ]
this aftos, aftee, afto [αυτός, αυτή, αυτό]
  this street aftos o thromos [αυτός ο δρόμος]
  this one afto etho [αυτό εδώ]
  is this ...? eene afto ...? [είναι αυτό ...;]
those *see* **these**
  no, not these, those! okhee, okhee afta,
  ekeena! [όχι, όχι αυτά, εκείνα!]
Thursday Pemtee [Πέμπτη]
ticket to eesseeteereeo [το εισιτήριο]
time: I haven't got time then ekho khrono [δεν
  έχω χρόνο] *see pages 124–125*
tired koorazmenos [κουρασμένος]
tissues khartomantheela [χαρτομάνδηλα]
to: to Crete ya teen Kreetee [για την Κρήτη]
today seemera [σήμερα]
together mazee [μαζί]
toilet ee tooaleta [η τουαλέτα]
tomorrow avreeo [αύριο]
  the day after tomorrow methavreeo
  [μεθαύριο]

tonight seemera to vrathee [σήμερα το βράδυ]
too polee [πολύ]; (also) epeessees [επίσης]
   that's too much afto eene para polee [αυτό
   είναι πάρα πολύ]
tour ee pereeotheea [η περιοδεία]
tourist o tooreestas [ο τουρίστας]
tourist office to grafeeo tooreezmoo [το γραφείο
   τουρισμού]
towel ee petseta [η πετσέτα]
town ee polee [η πόλη]
train to treno [το τραίνο]
translate metafrazo [μεταφράζω]
travel agency praktoreeo taxeetheeon [πρακτορείο
   ταξιδιών]
trousers to pandalonee [το πανταλόνι]
try thokeemazo [δοκιμάζω]
Tuesday Treetee [Τρίτη]
understand: I don't understand then
   katalaveno [δεν καταλαβαίνω]
urgent epeegon [επείγον]
us mas [μας]
use: can I use ...? boro na khreesseemopee-
   eesso ...? [μπορώ να χρησιμοποιήσω ...;]
vegetarian khortofagos [χορτοφάγος]
very polee [πολύ]
   very much para polee [πάρα πολύ]
village to khoreeo [το χωριό]
wait: I'm waiting for a friend pereemeno ena
   feelo [περιμένω ένα φίλο]
wake: will you wake me up at 7.30? boreete na
   me kseepneessete stees epta ke meessee?
   [μπορείτε να με ξυπνήσετε στις 7 και μισή;]
Wales Ooaleea [Ουαλλία]
want: I want a ... thelo ena ... [θέλω ένα ...]
   I don't want to then thelo [δεν θέλω]
warm khleearos [χλιαρός]
water to nero [το νερό]
we emees [εμείς]; **we are ...** eemaste ... [είμαστε]
Wednesday Tetartee [Τετάρτη]
week meea vthomatha [μιά βδομάδα]

well: how are you? – very well, thanks tee kanees? – polee kala efkhareesto [τί κάνεις; πολύ καλά ευχαριστώ]

wet eegros [υγρός]

what? tee? [τί;]

    what's that? tee eene ekeeno? [τί είναι εκείνο;]

when? pote? [πότε;]

where? poo? [πού;]

    where is ...? poo eene ...? [πού είναι;]

which? peeos? [ποιός;]

white aspro [άσπρο]

who? peeos? [ποιός;]

why? yatee? [γιατί;]

    why not? yatee okhee? [γιατί όχι;]

wife: my wife ee seezeegos moo [η σύζυγός μου]

window to paratheero [το παράθυρο]

windsurfing serf [σερφ]

wine to krassee [το κρασί]

with mazee [μαζί]

without khorees [χωρίς]

woman ee yeeneka [η γυναίκα]

work: it's not working then ergazete [δεν εργάζεται]

worry beads to komboloee [το κομπολόι]

write: could you write it down? boreeta na moo to grapsete? [μπορείτε να μου το γράψετε;]

wrong lathos [λάθος]

    there's something wrong with ... e-yeene kapeeo lathos me ... [έγινε κάποιο λάθος με]

    what's wrong? tee trekhee? [τί τρέχει;]

year o khronos [ο χρόνος]

yes ne [ναι]

yesterday khthes [χθες]

you essee [εσύ]; (*polite form*) essees [εσείς]

    are you ...? eesse .../eesthe ...? [г'σαι/είσθε ...;]

    with you mazee soo [μαζί σου'

young neos [νέος]

your theeko soo [δικό σου]

    (*polite form*) theeko sas [δικό σας]

youth hostel ksenonas neon [ξενώνας νέων]

0 meethen [μηδέν]
1 ena [ένα]
2 theeo [δύο]
3 treea [τρία]
4 tessera [τέσσερα]
5 pende [πέντε]
6 exee [έξι]
7 epta [επτά]
8 okto [οκτώ]
9 enea [εννέα]
10 theka [δέκα]

11 endeka [έντεκα]
12 thotheka [δώδεκα]
13 thekatreea [δεκατρία]
14 thekatessera [δεκατέσσερα]
15 thekapende [δεκαπέντε]
16 thekaexee [δεκαέξι]
17 thekaepta [δεκαεπτά]
18 thekaokto [δεκαοκτώ]
19 thekaenea [δεκαεννέα]
20 eekossee [είκοσι]
21 eekossee-ena [εικοσιένα]
22 eekossee-theeo [εικοσιδύο]
23 eekossee-treea [εικοσιτρία]
30 treeanda [τριάντα]
31 treeanda-ena [τριανταένα]
40 saranda [σαράντα]
50 peneenda [πενήντα]
60 exeenda [εξήντα]
70 evothmeenda [εβδομήντα]
80 ogthonda [ογδόντα]
90 eneneenda [ενενήντα]
100 ekato [εκατό]
101 ekaton ena [εκατόν ένα]
165 ekaton exeenda pende [εκατόν εξήντα πέντε]
200 theeakosseea [διακόσια]
300 treeakosseea [τριακόσια]
1,000 kheeleea [χίλια]
2,000 theeo kheeleeathes [δύο χιλιάδες]
4,655 tesserees kheeleeathes exakosseea
   peneenda pende

*for thousands use a full-stop: 3.000; for decimals a
comma: 4,6 ... koma ... [... κόμμα ...]*

ΟΡΕΚΤΙΚΑ   OREKTEEKA   APPETIZERS

Ντολμαδάκια Dolmathakeea
vine leaves stuffed with minced meat, rice and herbs

Μελιτζανοσαλάτα Meleedzanossalata
aubergine salad

Κεφτέδες Keftethes
meat balls

Ταραμοσαλάτα Taramossalata
fish roe pâté

Χταπόδι Khtapothee
boiled octopus

Σαλάτα χωριάτικη Salata khoreeateekee
mixed salad

Κοκορέτσι Kokoretsee
spit-roasted liver and innards

Τζατζίκι Dzadzeekee
a mixture of cucumber, yogurt and garlic

ΣΟΥΠΕΣ   SOOPES   SOUPS

Αυγολέμονο Avgolemono
chicken broth, lemon and egg

Κακαβιά Kakaveea
various kinds of fish

Πατσάς Patsas
intestines of lamb, washed and cut up

Φασολάδα Fassolatha
hot bean soup

MAIN DISHES

Στιφάδο Steefatho
hare or rabbit stew with onions

Μουσακάς Moussakas
layers of either aubergine or potatoes with minced meat topped with thick creamy sauce and baked

Γιουβαρλάκια Yoovarlakeea
minced meat, rice and seasoning in sauce

Παστίτσιο Pasteetseeo
  macaroni, minced meat and thick creamy sauce
Γιουβέτσι Yoovetsee
  roast lamb with pasta
Αρνί φρικασέ Arnee freekasse
  lamb, lettuce and thick white sauce
Αγκινάρες Ageenares
  artichokes in light sauce
Ντομάτες γεμιστές Domates yemeestes
  *tomatoes with a stuffing of minced meat, rice
  and herbs*
Πιπεριές γεμιστές Peeperee-es yemeestes
  stuffed green peppers
Λαχανοντολμάδες Lakhanodolmades
  cabbage leaves stuffed with rice and mince

ΘΑΛΑΣΣΙΝΑ THALASSEENA SEAFOOD

Μπακαλιάρος Bakaleearos
  cod, fried or boiled
Αστακός Astakos
  lobster, grilled or boiled
Γαρίδες Gareethes
  shrimps, grilled or boiled
Καλαμαράκια Kalamarakeea
  fried baby squid
Καβούρια Kavooreea
  boiled crab
Μύδια Meetheea
  mussels

ΓΛΥΚΑ GLEEKA DESSERTS

Καταίφι Kataeefee
  shredded pastry with nuts and honey
Μπακλαβάς Baklavas
  pastry filled with nuts and syrup
Λουκουμάδες Lookoomathes
  fritters coated in honey
Παγωτό Pagoto
  ice cream

what's the time?
French: quelle heure est-il? [kel urr ay-teel]
German: wie spät ist es? [vee shpayt ist ess]
Spanish: ¿que hora es? [keh ora ess]
Italian: che ore sono? [kay oh-ray ...]
Portuguese: que horas são? [kee orush sowng]
Greek: tee ora eene? [τί ώρα είναι;]

it's one o'clock
F: il est une heure [eel ay oon urr]
G: es ist ein Uhr [ess ist ine oor]
S: es la una
I: è l'una [eh ...]
P: é uma hora [eh oomuh oruh]
Gk: eene meea ee ora [είναι μία η ώρα]

it's two/three/four o'clock
F: il est deux/trois/quatre heures
G: es ist zwei/drei/vier Uhr
S: son las dos/tres/cuatro
I: sono le due/tre/quattro
P: são duas/três/quatro horas
Gk: eene theeo/trees/tesserees ee ora
 [είναι δύο/τρεις/τέσσερεις η ώρα]

five/twenty past six
F: six heures cinq/vingt
G: fünf/zwanzig nach sechs [... nahk ...]
S: las seis y cinco/veinte [... ee ...]
I: le sei e cinque/venti [... eh ...]
P: seis e cinco/vinte [... ee ...]
Gk: exee ke pende/eekossee [έξι και
 πέντε/είκοσι]

quarter past seven
F: sept heures et quart [... kahr]
G: Viertel nach sieben [feer-tel ...]
S: las siete y cuarto [... kwartoh]
I: le sette e un quarto [... kwartoh]
P: sete e um quarto [... kwartoo]
Gk: epta ke tetarto [επτά και τέταρτο]

....

half past eight
F: huit heures et demi [... duh-mee]
G: halb neun [halp ...]
S: las ocho y media [... maid-ya]
I: le otto e mezza [... met-tzah]
P: oito e meia [... mayuh]
Gk: okto ke meesee [οκτώ και μισή]

ten/five to nine
F: neuf heures moins dix/cinq [... mwāñ ...]
G: zehn/fünf vor neun
S: las nueve menos diez/cinco [... meh-noss ...]
I: le nove meno dieci/cinque [... may-noh ...]
P: dez menos dez/cinco [... meh-noosh ...]
Gk: enea para theka/pende
[εννέα παρά δέκα/πέντε]

quarter to ten
F: dix heures moins le quart
G: Viertel vor zehn
S: las diez menos cuarto
I: le dieci meno un quarto
P: dez menos um quarto
Gk: theka para tetarto [δέκα παρά τέταρτο]

midday
F: midi [mee-dee]
G: Mittag [mittahg]
S: mediodía [mehd-yoh-dee-a]
I: mezzogiorno [met-tzo-jor-noh]
P: meio-dia [mayoo-dee-uh]
Gk: messeemeree [μεσημέρι]

midnight
F: minuit [mee-nwee]
G: Mitternacht [mitter-nahkt]
S: medianoche [meh-dee-ah-notcheh]
I: mezzanotte [met-tza-not-tay]
P: meia-noite [mayuh-noyt]
Gk: messaneekta [μεσάνυχτα]

....

bust measurements

UK:	32	34	36	38	40
Euro:	80	87	91	97	102

centigrade
conversion: $C \div 5 \times 9 + 32 = F$

centigrade:	−5	0	10	15	21	30	36.9
Fahrenheit:	23	32	50	59	70	86	98.4

centimetres 1 cm = 0.39 inches

chest measurements

UK:	34	36	38	40	42	44	46
Euro:	87	91	97	102	107	112	117

collar sizes

UK (*old*):	14	14½	15	15½	16	16½	17
Euro:	36	37	38	39	41	42	43

dress sizes

UK:	10	12	14	16	18	20
Euro:	38	40	42	44	46	48

French and Greek sizes: for 38 read 36 etc

Fahrenheit
conversion: $F - 32 \times 5 \div 9 = C$

Fahrenheit:	23	32	50	59	70	86	98.4
centigrade:	−5	0	10	15	21	30	36.9

feet 1 foot = 30.1 cm = 0.3 metres

gallons 1 gallon = 4.55 litres

inches 1 inch = 2.54 cm

kilos
conversion: $kilos \div 5 \times 11 = pounds$

kilos:	1	1½	5	6	7	8	9
pounds:	2.2	3.3	11	13.2	15.4	17.6	19.8

kilometres
conversion: $kilometres \div 8 \times 5 = miles$

kilometres:	1	5	10	20	50	100
miles:	0.62	3.11	6.2	12.4	31	62

litres 1 litre = 1 pint = 0.22 galls

metres 1 metre=39.37 ins=1.09 yds

miles
conversion: miles÷5×8=kilometres

miles:	0.5	1	3	5	10	50	100
kilometres:	0.8	1.6	4.8	8	16	80	160

pints 1 pint=0.57 litres

pounds
conversion: pounds÷11×5=kilos

pounds:	1	3	5	6	7	8	9
kilos:	0.45	1.4	2.3	2.7	3.2	3.6	4.1

shoe sizes

UK:	4	5	6	7	8	9	10	11
Euro:	37	38	39	41	42	43	44	46

stones 1 stone=6.35 kilos

tons 1 ton=1,016 kilos

tyre pressures

lb/sq in:	18	20	22	24	26	28	30
kg/sq in:	1.3	1.4	1.5	1.7	1.8	2	2.1

waist measurements

UK:	24	26	28	30	32	34	36	38
Euro:	61	66	71	76	80	87	91	97

yards 1 yard=91.44 cm=0.91 m

MONEY

France:	**franc** un franc [fron] 100 centimes [son-teem]=F1
Germany:	**mark** eine Mark; (*5 marks* fünf Mark); 100 Pfennig=DM1
Spain:	**pesetas** pesetas [peh-seh-tass] 100 céntimos [then-teemoss]=una peseta
Italy:	**lire** lire [lee-ray]
Portugal:	**escudos** escudos [shkoodoosh] 100 centavos=1$ (um escudo)
Greece:	**drachmas** drakhmes [δραχμές]